MARTYN LEWIS

cats in the news

Macdonald
Illustrated

To the irreplaceable Yang,
The Roo, Possum, Charger
and all cats with their spirit.

A Macdonald Illustrated Book

© Limar Enterprises 1991

First issued in Great Britain by Macdonald Illustrated
a division of
Macdonald & Co (Publishers) Ltd
165 Great Dover Street
London SE1 4YA

A member of Maxwell Macmillan Pergamon Publishing Corporation

British Cataloguing in Publication Data
Lewis, Martyn
Cats in the News
I. Title
828

ISBN 0 356 20282 8

Made by Lennard Associates Ltd
Mackerye End, Harpenden, Herts AL5 5DR

Design by COOPER WILSON
Jacket design by Pocknell & Co
Jacket photograph by Kim Sayer

Printed and bound in England by
The Bath Press, Bath, Avon.

CONTENTS

Acknowledgements

In addition to the cats and their owners, without whom this book would not have been possible, I would like to thank the editors of the news services which reported the stories and the photographers who tracked down the personalities and in many cases reconstructed the events.

I am also grateful to Kim Sayer for his excellent portrait of Rosie for the jacket, to Suzanne O'Farrell for her diligent researching of many of the other photographs, to Alison Bravington and Michael Leitch for their editorial support and to Paul Cooper, Marie Chung and Barry Yeomans for assembling the book both attractively and fast, so retrieving much of the time lost by the late delivery of the manuscript!

Thanks too for some splendid illustrations provided by Hector Breeze, Ian Dicks, David Haldane, John Ireland, Edward McLachlan, Rob Shone and Colin Whittock.

Finally a special thank you to my wife Liz for her tolerance and support of my late nights at the word processor and to Rosie who was a constant muse.

Picture Acknowledgements

The publishers would like to thank the following sources for their permission to reproduce copyright material. Where there is more than one picture on a page the pictures are numbered a,b,c etc from the top of the page.
Associated Press 15a; Associated Press/Topham 127; Paul Bella/Frank Spooner Pictures/Gamma 18; Roger Bull/Frank Spooner Pictures/Gamma 75; Colchester Zoo 11; A.Dawson 38b; Mary Evans Picture Library 39b, 69a, 69b, 89, 116; The Hulton-Deutsch Collection 20a, 20b, 30, 33b, 41a, 41b, 44, 56a, 60, 63, 75, 77a, 77b, 81, 86, 90b, 93b, 96, 98, 100, 114a, 114b, 117, 118, 122, 123, 128, 129a, 130, 133, 135b, 142a, 142b; Illustrated London News Picture Library 97, 125a, 125b, 126; Sichikawa Kwita/Frank Spooner Pictures 148; Popperfoto 8, 14, 22a, 22b, 38a, 50a, 52, 65, 66, 73, 87, 90a, 92, 99, 109a, 111, 129b, 134a, 134b, 135a, 138, 141, 144, 151; Press Association/Topham 121; Retna Pictures 61, 101; Rex Features 15b, 122a; Rex Features/Sipa 107; Saatchi & Saatchi 57; Eric Sander/Frank Spooner Pictures/Gamma 39a; Solo Syndication 46; Frank Spooner Pictures/Gamma 75; Syndication International 7, 12, 13a, 13b, 23, 24, 27, 28a, 28b, 32, 33a, 36, 37, 42a, 42b, 45, 47, 56b, 57, 64, 72, 76, 80, 82, 83, 84a, 84b, 91, 93a, 93c, 95, 102a, 102b, 103, 109b, 110, 112, 113, 115, 119a, 119b, 145, 146, 147, 149, 150, 152; Times Newspapers 10; Topham Picture Library 120, 128b.

INTRODUCTION

If you love cats, you will almost certainly have – or have had – one which dominated your life. In my case she was a magnificent silky Siamese who arrived as a tiny bundle already rejoicing in the name of Paiwaket Yang Hi Yu Fing Ming. She was decent enough not to complain when we quickly and unceremoniously shortened it to Yang – effectively abandoning public recognition of her splendid pedigree.

Yang rode shot-gun to my days of growing up. From as far back as I can remember – to several years after I left for university – she dominated our house with a love that far transcended the routine mealtime affections. She became, in our judgment, as human as any animal can be, delivering friendship and understanding by the bowlful. She would hold long, detailed conversations with my mother, curled lazily and happily across the back of her shoulders like a shawl as she busied herself around the house – offering advice, and pouring out tales of her night-time adventures. She proudly laid out mice and birds on our back step like food parcels, as though the very act of catching them had been in response to *our* needs rather than *her* natural instincts.

. She occasionally erred – climbing onto the table to polish off the cream left at the bottom of what had been a particularly fine sherry trifle – an escapade only revealed by an unsteady walk induced by her underestimation of the generous amount of alcohol with which my mother was wont to lace her puddings.

Yang was always forgiven. In return, if any of us felt badly done by, or momentarily lonely and in need of a friend, she would *never* let you down.

It was years before I could accept another cat of my own again – before I was prepared to risk the inevitable comparisons. Perhaps that was a mistake. After little more than a year, a British Silver

Tabby called Rosie has entrenched herself in the affections of another generation of the Lewis family. Skittish to be chased, melting into a soft miaow when caught, she is on her way to a Yang-like eminence in our lives. As all cat-loving families have found, cats are indeed catalysts – mellowing human moods, perceptibly changing the impression and atmosphere of any room they have chosen to inhabit. They contribute immeasurably to the lives of countless people, to whom they are friends and confidants. They become human – and like all humans they do things that are out of the ordinary – things that make news.

For years now, I have quietly collected – from newspapers and television – some of the more extraordinary cat achievements, mistakes and escapades. It was but a short, delightful step from that to a more thorough combing of the many occasions when cats have hit the headlines around the world over the last century or so; and I have had immense pleasure in knitting together the best of those stories in this book. I do so as a tribute to the resilience and ingenuity of our feline friends; and as a necessary antidote to the inevitable seriousness of my professional life – a way of tipping my hat to those enjoyably lighter stories which are quite properly squeezed out of the national TV News programmes I usually inhabit by the sheer weight of vastly more important news. It is also this newscaster's small personal way of trying to make amends for not always being able to bring you quite as much good news as I would like.

Martyn Lewis,
Kensington,
London W8.
1991

CURIOUS CATS

According to the "cat bible" kept in Thailand's national museum, six centuries ago there were no fewer than seventeen breeds of Siamese cat. Now thirteen of them are extinct, and, claim the purists, the rich colours of the four remaining original breeds - seal point, blue, copper and white - have paled or muddied in other countries. That claim raises hackles amongst those Western cat lovers and breeders for whom pedigree (interestingly, a Western invention) is all-important. They treat their cats with a reverence akin to those early days in Thailand, when the elegant animals were kept in palaces on the assumption that "cats were for the higher classes, while the common people had dogs". And so there is a constant quest not only to retain the purity of the existing thirty-seven species of the cat family, but to develop and nurture new ones as well. Not surprisingly, such efforts carry the cats and their owners into the national spotlight.

"Cats were for the higher classes, while the common people had dogs."

The birth of five perfect Korat kittens at the London home of Mrs Anne Marie Locher made headlines because such cats are rarely seen outside their native Thailand. Their distinctive big ears, large feet and huge emerald eyes have remained unchanged from those described in an ancient 400-year-old book, making them probably the purest, most unadapted breed of cat in the world today. The explanation lies in the common belief that they are endowed with all manner of magical, lucky qualities - so for many years the

Two of the Korat kittens bred by Mrs Anne Marie Locher.

kittens were never sold for money, but were only *given* away to mark very special occasions such as weddings or births. That changed in 1959 when the first Korats for breeding were imported into the United States. Thirteen years later they arrived in Britain - in the form of a litter born in quarantine. Their gracefulness is reminiscent of the Siamese, their friendliness and affection for people knows no bounds, and the silver tips on their hairs create the charming impression of a cat which has played in a tubful of stardust - a combination of qualities which ensure that their pedigree is jealously guarded. Even today they remain one of the rare jewels of the cat world - an honour they share with the sacred Temple Cats of Burma.

The silver tips on their hairs create the charming impression of a cat which has played in a tubful of stardust.

Known as Birmans, these produced their first British litter - no fewer than eight - for Mrs Elsie Fischer of Hampstead in 1966. Legend has it that the original temple cat turned into gold when its master was killed - except for its feet, which remained pure white.

It was a Birman's liaison with an Angora called Josephine that produced a whole new breed of cat - the Ragdoll - officially recognised by Britain's National Cat Club in 1987. But the Ragdoll's appearance is believed to have been influenced in some mysterious way by a car accident. For it was after being struck by a car that Josephine produced a litter of positively enormous kittens with singularly angelic, placid and intelligent dispositions. They are called Ragdolls because if you pick one up and cuddle it, it will loll back in your

All eight Birman kittens pose for the family album.

8

arms like a baby - only they're a great deal heavier: the females can weigh up to fifteen pounds, the males as much as twenty. Grace McHattie, former Editor of the magazine *Cat World*, says they're like a herd of elephants - "I've heard mine coming upstairs and thought it was someone trying to break in." She finds hers almost as easy to train as dogs - "They come not only when called, but when you whistle; and the kittens play like puppies, chasing things you throw for them." Critics have suggested that because Ragdolls appear not to feel pain, they risk being hugged to death by children, that you can't tell when they're ill, and that they're so lethargic they won't run away from danger. Owners will have none of that - they're simply happy to own a cat whose size alone has won it a place in the *Guinness Book of Records*.

Two cats in Los Angeles were just as happy to settle for the Neiman-Marcus 1986 Christmas catalogue. This world-famous speciality company that once offered "His" and "Hers" personal submarines had no problem charging $1400 apiece for cats they called "a completely new breed of American domestic feline". Put on display at the Neiman Beverley Hills store, the two animals were soon drawing the crowds. Bullseye was a grey male kitten with black spots, and Cucamonga a deep red female with black stripes and spots. They were the brainchild of West Coast breeder Paul Casey, also a Hollywood writer equally at home turning out scripts for such TV series as *Lassie* and *Banacek*. There was no centuries-old pedigree behind Bullseye and Cucamonga - it took Casey just fifteen years of clever cross-breeding to produce what the purists would call rather unusual moggies. He started with a cat of the Nile from Africa and crossed it with a Malayan tropical house cat - two breeds which, he claimed, "had not been together in 100,000 years!" Along the way Casey added Siamese, Angora and Abyssinians to the equation, producing markings which, he said, made them like no others cats in the

> *"I've heard mine coming upstairs and thought it was someone trying to break in."*

world. That may have been true, but there are plenty of other cats waiting to lay claim to that title in their own way!

Take the Maine Coon, for example - which is something American families seem to be doing in growing numbers. These cats from New England behave like dogs, and actually like water - some to the extent of "sitting in sinks waiting for mice to emerge from the plughole!" Their tails can be as long as their bodies, which have thick, downy fur on their bellies, and long hairs almost like plumes on top. History gives the Maine Coon a highly romantic past, although some of it may be more myth than fact. One theory is that they were taken to America by the Vikings four hundred years before the arrival of Columbus, and are a cross between a cat and a raccoon or a cat and a lynx. An even more curious legend makes them descendants of Marie Antoinette's favourite cats, which were shipped to the United States (along with her belongings) and left to fend for themselves. At any rate, they were the first show cats in the USA, taking part in exhibitions in Maine as early as the 1860s.

Smoky, the Maine Coon, goes shopping.

One of their breed, named Smoky, went so far as to grace the pages of an early edition of the London *Times* in May 1987. Perched on his mistress's shoulders, he apparently insisted on going along for the ride whenever she went shopping. The newspaper's report, which detailed Smoky's devotion to sinks, provoked a mildly irate letter in its correspondence columns a few days later, proving that journalists who make claims about cats are venturing into sensitive territory. A Mr M.T. McGrave of Winchester wrote admonishingly: "Sir, An attachment to sinks is *not* peculiar to Maine Coon cats. My pedigree-

**"Sir,
An attachment to
sinks is not
peculiar to Maine
Coon cats."**

less cat loves to sit in a sink. I have always supposed he was waiting for fish to emerge from the tap."

One very rare breed of cat isn't prepared to wait even a second for its fish - it dives in to catch them. The Asian Fishing Cat (Felis Viverinus), about twice the size and weight of a domestic moggy, has a reputation for being utterly fearless. It will happily take on animals very much bigger than itself, and one is even known to have killed a leopard. More routinely, it uses its strangely webbed feet to swim under water to catch its daily meals. Found in remote forests and marshlands of Asia, many of which are threatened by human development projects, it is now an endangered species. Colchester Zoo is one of the few places looking after its interests, successfuly breeding them in captivity. Their first male kitten, Columbo, was rejected by his mother immediately he was born, and was hand-

*They will happily take
on animals much bigger
than themselves, and one
is even known to have
killed a leopard.*

Columbo,
Colchester's
fearless fisherman.

reared by the zoo director Angela Tropeano. Milk, administered every three hours, sustained him through the first eight weeks until he showed an appetite for more solid food. With no signs of the breed's reputed shyness, Columbo is said to be "full of energy, very extrovert, and enjoying human companionship so he can practise fighting and biting!" The zoo managed

Fun in the bath for
Bean and Sprout.

to breed another three Asian Fishing Cats early in 1991, and they are all proving a great attraction.

Not quite so rare, but still unusual enough to make occasional headlines, are the once wild Turkish Swimming Cats, now domesticated enough to make lively pets for anyone who doesn't mind trails of water all through the house. Early British breeders included Mrs Florence Bond in the Derbyshire village of Heanor, who found that mothers lost no time in introducing their kittens to the children's paddling pool in the back garden. After just a few lengths grimly clinging onto Mum, the kittens were ready to strike out on their own. And after that, any stretch of water is fair game! Nine-month-old Catriona Lazenby took great delight in insisting that two of them (ten-week-old twins Bean and Sprout) joined her for bathtime at their home in Macclesfield in Cheshire. Catriona's mother, Lorna, wasn't so sure - she had to clear up the mess afterwards.

While combing the world for rare breeds of cat is a splendid (and often lucrative) pastime, there is nothing quite like the satisfaction of producing a homegrown model - and every so often, by accident or design, a new and unusual animal will emerge. The Devon Rex has hogged more than its fair share of the limelight since its début less than thirty years ago. With ears like Dumbo the elephant, a face like a pixie's, and a tightly curled coat, it is a photographer's delight. Considering that even by 1969 there were reckoned to be only fifty of them in the world, they have an uncanny capacity to come up with new reasons for hitting the headlines. Mrs Glenda Worthy of Hoddesdon in Hertfordshire bred twins whose white coats were sprinkled exotically with lilac

Mrs Glenda Worthy's pixie-faced twins.

highlights. And the entertainer, Rolf Harris, once had no fewer than seven Devon Rexes running around his home in Kent. His camera captured one of them - named rather unflatteringly "Ratbag" - in a rather appealing pose, but when the picture was printed Rolf saw, to his amazement, the unmistakable features of a man's head on his cat's right ear. A trick of the light, perhaps, but there were plenty of people who thought it gave more than a little "paws" for thought.

Ben, who may have had difficulty explaining his tortoiseshell markings to other tomcats!

Occasionally, of course, things can go wrong with the breeding process, producing feline freaks like a blue tortoiseshell Devon Rex called Ben, owned by Mrs Roma Lund of Maidenhead. By all the laws of nature, *he* should be a *she*. Only female cats can have tortoiseshell markings - except when genetic accidents happen. And the odds against producing a tortoiseshell tomcat are more than a million-to-one. That made Ben worth almost a thousand pounds at today's prices - but Mrs Lund had no intention of selling him. "To me," she said, "he's just a lovable and very affectionate cat."

Back in 1956, five years of scientific breeding on the Cornish Moors produced another kind of curly cat - one with an Astrakhan coat and a thin walrus moustache. Shaped like hares, and with fur in shades of apricot and grey, they were the work of Mrs Nina Ennismore and her cousin Miss Winifred McAllister. They made sure their cats led a sheltered life in heated huts and wired-off runs, and they didn't snarl - presumably because they never saw anything to snarl at. But some attempts to breed cats with curly coats can produce kittens which are bald - nude cats, as they are often called. Without some human help they would be wiped out by a cold winter. Two lucky ones were Starkers and Baldy, well looked after in 1970 by Suzanne

A fine Astrakhan coat for this curly cat.

Bicknell at the Blue Cross Animal Hospital in London's Victoria. Their picture so attracted the *Daily Mirror* that they broke their rule about never allowing nudes onto their pages!

Over the next sixteen years or so, someone clearly decided to make hairless cats less of an accident, because one turned up at an animal show in New York, with its owner claiming he knew of a hundred more in various locations around the world. What really attracted the photographers was the cat's remarkable resemblance to the

Some attempts to breed cats with curly coats can produce kittens which are bald - nude cats, as they are often called.

Gremlins, those cuddly creatures that turned into movie monsters. With such an extraordinary appearance, it was inevitable that someone would find a more mysterious explanation for their existence. A French antique dealer, Patrick Challan, attempting to revive them as a breed, speculated that they were Sphinx cats, which lived in China in ancient times, and resulted from a strange liaison between a cat and a "beautiful midget hairless dog"! He noted that his five nude cats were never afraid of dogs, approaching them in a friendly fashion wanting to play. Monsieur Challan's research also found that somehow such cats had padded into the writings of a few English authors, and had

Gizmo, a sphinx cat from Paris, meets the rather more traditional ragdoll who had just won best of breed at the 1986 International Cat Show in New York.

been sighted in Canada just after the country was conquered by the British. Such speculation about just when these cats had laid their paws on history inevitably upped their market value. An American offered Monsieur Challan fifty thousand dollars for his five nude cats. The offer was rejected, the Frenchman having ambitions of

Two of Monsieur Challan's cats, looking sadly naked.

his own to turn the animals into a modern breed of domestic cat. There is no sign that he has succeeded on any large scale, and many cat-lovers will be grateful that they have been spared a mass invasion by such patently ugly cats.

The only other cats associated vaguely with baldness were brought into national prominence by RSPCA inspectors in Birmingham. They were appalled that some owners in the city were shaving bald patches on their animals, dyeing what fur was left all kinds of bright colours, and even fitting ear studs! Fortunately, such "designer" cats don't seem to have caught on.

One skirmish about cats was even fought out in the august columns of *The Times*. Bernard Levin, in devoting one of his regular columns to his passionate love of cats, innocently threw out an aside which aroused a great deal of passion, if not outright anger. "In all my life," he wrote, "I do not think I have met as many as half a dozen cats I did not like. True, I have taken care to keep out of the way of Chinchillas, the only breed ugly in themselves...." And, in reviewing a favourite book on cats, he went on to highlight one particular Long-Haired-White Chinchilla which "looks simply nasty - a feat almost literally impossible for a cat". *The Times*'s Letters Page soon reverberated with a firm repudiation from no

less a person than the Chairman of the United Chinchilla Association. Mr M.J. Turney wrote indignantly, "The Association very much resents the comments made concerning a breed renowned for its beauty and ethereal qualities. To substantiate this, I enclose a photo of the most recent winning male Chinchilla, Grand Champion Snowbloom Jabin - owned and bred by Mrs K. Evans of Westcliff-on-Sea. This cat has won 18 Challenge certificates, four Grand Championships, six Reserve Grand Championships and, at last year's show held by the Governing Council of the Cat Fancy, was awarded Supreme Best Exhibit in Show which, I think, proves the worth of this breed. The Association would appreciate publication of the enclosed photo so that your readers may assess for themselves the truth in Mr Levin's article." The photograph duly appeared beside the published letter. As for Mr Levin, faced with the combined wrath of the cat world, he wisely chose to remain uncharacteristically silent.

Some owners in the city were shaving bald patches on their animals, dyeing what fur was left all kinds of bright colours, and even fitting ear studs!

No criticism tolerated, then, over the Chinchilla - but a mighty row about another breed, the Scottish Fold, has rumbled on through the cat world for years. It all began in 1961 when a shepherd, William Ross, crossing a remote farmyard in Perthshire, noticed a small, white female cat with drooping - or folded - ears. He asked the farmer if he could have one of her kittens, and went on to breed them, usually mating a Fold with a normal-eared, short-haired cat. William had some help from geneticists, who concluded that the cats' ears were the result of a single dominant gene. Although particularly popular in the United States, where they are now most widely bred, the Scottish Folds at first upset the more purist of cat lovers, who found them "aesthetically and biologically unacceptable", and claimed that the drooping ears became a dirt-

The Scottish Fold, with its distinctly flattened look, makes a first appearance at the Paris Cat Show in 1982.

trap, encouraging parasites and deafness. For that reason they were, at first, banned from competitions. But as the breed developed it became clear that they were, in fact, extremely resistant to disease. Add to that their hardiness, affection, peacefulness and sociability, and it is not difficult to see why, in 1978, they were finally allowed into the privileged world of American cat shows - and four years later one even made it to the Paris Cat Show. But for years, the governing council of Britain's Cat Fancy (the feline equivalent of the Kennel Club) tried to outlaw the Scottish Fold, and even issued special instructions to make sure it did not "taint" the National Cat Club's Centenary show at London's Olympia in 1987. Imagine their horror and embarrassment when the kitten which walked off with top rosette in the "Any Other Varieties" section, was revealed to be a dreaded Scottish Fold. The chairman of the Governing Council promptly blamed it on "the inexperience of the judge in a class that attracts little attention, and the fact that a Scottish Fold kitten's ears are not immediately noticeable" (they don't start to bend for about four weeks). *Cat Magazine* stepped into the controversy, declaring that breeders had agreed "the massive cobby type, round head and short coat of the British Short-Hair, as seen in the first Scottish Folds, should be preserved". And attempted to end the controversy by pointing out that "whatever one's aesthetic reactions to the Scottish Fold, its selective breeding is certainly no more objectionable than that of some accepted Persian pedigrees with noses so short that they can hardly breathe!"

WORKING CATS

In the days when greyhound racing fans flocked to London's White City track, they little knew that they came under the protection of one formidable female tabby. Legend has it that she tracked down and killed 12,480 rats during her six years in charge of the stadium's rodent control programme. The annual catch wasn't quite so impressive in a distillery at Glen Turret on Tayside – but then Towser stuck at the job rather longer, making it a lifetime commitment. In twenty-four years of prowling, he produced 28,899 mice – an average of three a day – all proudly laid at the feet of the delighted managers. It matters not that most cats would happily give a paw and a leg to have such rich hunting grounds. These feline caretakers are still classified as belonging to the great world-wide army of "working cats". If cats could talk,

In twenty-four years of prowling, he produced 28,899 mice.

MICK THE MILLER

TABBY THE KILLER

McLACHLAN

19

A reluctant mouser about to be press-ganged into service.

they would undoubtedly express utter amazement that an instinctive activity which they regard as one of the great pleasures in life is considered something of a chore by humans who really ought to know better. Still, they are not beyond taking full advantage of this strange lapse on the part of their masters and mistresses.

In 1938 a large store in London's Oxford Street was over-run by mice. An emergency call went out to the District Messengers' office – headquarters for the Thirties' equivalent of today's motorbike-borne dispatch riders – and, on foot, the messengers set out to round up every cat they could find and deliver them to the unfortunate shopowners.

During the Second World War, the Ministry of Supply organised a special call-up for cats – recruiting them for the war on mice and rats in Britain's secret food dumps. Pet shops were designated as central collecting points, and shopkeepers like George Palmer of Camden Town reported felines arriving at the

Cats by the handful on their way to the Ministry of Supply.

rate of a hundred a day, as the cat-owners of Britain patriotically brought in their animals to serve King and Country. Said Mr Palmer: "So long as they are capable of mousing [and one wonders what cat is not!], I buy them for between two and five shillings apiece, and sell them to the Ministry for a little more."

An official working for the American Department of Agriculture had the nerve to question whether cats were really effective in tackling rats. After conducting a survey of farms in Massachusetts, Edward H. Forbush concluded that while cats *were* pretty effective in polishing off mice, their track record with rats was little short of disastrous. "Absolutely worthless for the purpose" was his insulting verdict; and he went on to argue that cats did not destroy enough rodents to compensate for the damage they did to wildlife, particularly to birds. Against that stands the testimony of a Michigan farmer whose cat was in the habit of bringing its catch into the house. Over eighteen months, its hunting tally added up to sixteen hundred mice, twenty-three other small mammals, and only sixty-two birds. On the whole, researchers agree that cats eat more rodents than birds, but they

Fluffy saved him hours of work hauling up carpets and boards by running under floors with new cable attached to his collar.

disagree about the proportions. Some say birds account for twenty-five per cent of their diet; others put it as low as four per cent. But those figures apply to domestic cats that have gone wild. With more home-loving cats the bird count is probably in direct proportion to the number of tins of cat-food opened. So it seems reasonable to assume that such statistics will vary from place to place and cat to cat, according to the hunting opportunities on offer.

Occasionally there appear working cats not motivated solely by the tug of the wild or the call of the tummy. In 1982, Aberdeen electrician Ian Murdoch revealed that his moggy, Fluffy, saved him hours of work hauling up carpets and boards by running under floors with new cable attached to his collar. Ian said the cat enjoyed his job so much he sulked if the van left for work in the morning without him. Not so Felix, who was left lashing his tail in protest after his owners, the French government, gave him the last job on earth any cat would willingly do. They sent him into space on board an experimental rocket in 1963, with various electronic

Felix is none too happy with his role as a guinea pig in space.

devices attached to his brain to monitor how he coped with the high life. After that he, not surprisingly, opted for early retirement, and was sent to pad around the Natural History Museum at Vincennes, perhaps uncertain whether he was there as a mouser or an exhibit!

Four years later, Tiger had no such doubts when he was taken on by the Lockheed Propulsion Company's test facility at Potrero in California. His job was to help technician Harry Herbert keep the main control complex – and the tunnels beneath it – free of wire-chewing mice who regularly caused annoying delays and expensive damage. You may think Tiger was about as low-tech as you can get, but Lockheed reckoned his speed of response was faster than any computer, and that over the years he would prove highly cost-effective, saving them twenty-five thousand dollars in his lifetime.

Lockheed's Tiger – low-tech but high productivity.

Most working cats seem to be able to negotiate a good deal for themselves without any help; but some call in a trade union to look after their interests. In 1986, Smudge was issued with a union card when he was appointed official Rat Catcher at Glasgow's People's Palace Museum. He happily proved his loyalty by wearing the card around his neck; but there were some who questioned whether he would have the self-discipline to toe the line if the union called a work-to-rule! In Blackburn, the council officers' union, NALGO, took the trouble to find a retirement house for one of its members – ace rat-catcher Pele, who had kept the local council's Darwen Road depot rodent-

Smudge was issued with a union card when he was appointed official Rat Catcher at Glasgow's People's Palace Museum.

free for seventeen years. As well as advertising for a new home, the union started a campaign to save Pele from the dole, arguing that even though he'd been given his marching orders, his particular talents were still worthy of a slightly less demanding market.

Compensation for another sacked cat, Jerry, came in the shape of a ten pound note. She was among two hundred and fifty workers who picked up redundancy pay when a brass and copper strip factory closed down in the Midlands. Prepared to work virtually twenty-four hours a day, the rat-catcher had been on the payroll all her life, and wasn't terribly familiar with the big world outside. Maintenance

Pele faces up to unemployment.

engineer Harold Green showed Jerry the way out – and found her a new home with Worsley Animal Rescue.

Nine-week-old Candy nearly caused a big union bust-up when she signed on as the new mouser at Bradford City Hall. Her fur colour and markings made her a natural for the white-collar union NALGO. But within weeks, some of her union colleagues were calling for her to be booted out. They said Candy didn't have the "managerial style" of her predecessor, Lucky, who'd disappeared. And they went on to argue that since Candy's duties were mainly manual, she was in the wrong union – and should have joined NUPE, the National Union of Public Employees. NUPE hit back, arguing that NALGO should never have taken the cat on in the first place.

Candy, the cat who lacked the skills necessary for membership of NALGO.

But any inter-union rivalry was put in the shade by the British Veterinary Association, which in 1981 described working cats as "oppressed workers", and called for their conditions of employment to be improved. Its official spokeman revealed that the "silent majority" of working cats plied their profession in granaries, aircraft hangars, theatres, factories, fashion houses and stores. "Their job," he said, "is to reduce food wastage, control rodent contamination, protect electrical installations against sabotage, and thus save on fire and insurance claims. Their modest return for this work is often just

FELLOW WORKERS!....

one meal a day and a warm place to sleep. But, like other workers,"
he went on, "they have their off days. They get flu, enteritis, fleas
and worms, and frequently the females have unwanted pregnancies.
But there is neither danger money nor much sympathy – even
though the cost of maintaining feline staff can be a tax-deductible
expense". It wasn't long before this particular "cat-call" was
answered.

Myra Hammond formed "Cats In Industry", a Sheffield-based
charity dedicated to improving conditions for an estimated half a
million homeless cats who, she insisted, didn't get a decent deal
from many factory managements. Some working cats, she claimed,
suffered appalling neglect, living in dirty and dangerous conditions
with little food. So she and a volunteer helper went into plants and
factories "trespassing where necessary", she admits, and arranging
veterinary care for any cat that needed it. She lobbied managements

to set up proper feeding systems and vaccination programmes for stray cats in their factories, and where that failed she contacted workers direct – "trying to recruit union members who will look after the cats and adopt unhappy ones by taking them home. It's a misconception," she said, "that all these cats are wild and can't be domesticated. They just need time to get accustomed to a new environment, and, after a period, they usually adjust to life in an ordinary home very well." "Cats In Industry" was soon running small shelters in several areas, including Middlesbrough, Southampton and South Wales; and Myra Hammond had taken voluntary redundancy from her job as an industrial journalist to become its full-time organiser.

"It's a misconception," she said, "that all these cats are wild and can't be domesticated."

Before long, she had five hundred people paying two pounds a year subscription, and donating gifts ranging from food for the cats to jewelry and clothes for fund-raising sales. Although a strong campaigner for having factory cats spayed to control their breeding, she realised that industry might think some sixteen pounds a cat to be on the expensive side. So, when last hitting the headlines, "Cats In Industry" was experimenting with an alternative – slipping its cats contraceptive pills disguised in pieces of sausage.

The Times Diary reported with some incredulity that Myra's address at the time (1982) was Tom Lane, Sheffield.

STAYING ALIVE

I t was some time before anyone in the Anderton family noticed that Midge, one of their four-month-old Siamese kittens, was missing. They searched for twenty-four hours without success, until someone thought of looking in the attic, where the winter temperature was well below that in the warm, comfortable house below. Midge was lying there, apparently cold and lifeless – until Mrs Joan Anderton thought of the kiss of life. "I breathed into her for more than half an hour," she said, "and then put her on a hot water bottle." Midge made a full recovery – but Mrs Anderton did not explain how she held the kitten's nose while giving it mouth-to-mouth resuscitation, or what it felt like to wrap her lips tightly around a cat's furry mouth.

"I breathed into her for more than half an hour," she said, "and then put her on a hot water bottle."

When Max the cat fell seriously ill in Brighton in 1985, his owner, Mrs Ann Howick, took him along to the local vet, Jonathan Gravestock, who carried out the kind of operation that is still extremely rare in the animal world – a blood transfusion. Step forward Max's sister, Miller! Although not exactly asked if she was willing to give blood, she appeared pretty pleased with the result when the two cats were reunited in Mrs Howick's arms. Max went on to make a full recovery, probably unaware·of the full extent of his sister's devotion – or of his own place in cat history.

Brighton is clearly one of the best places for unusual cat operations. Six years earlier,

Joan Anderton demonstrates the technique which saved Midge's life

Max and Miller, his
blood-donor sister.

John and Chris Moulton were distraught when their four-year-old tabby, Tigger, was almost killed in a car accident. They decided to rebuild him – well, not all of him – just one of his back legs, which had been pretty badly smashed up. John and Chris forked out a hundred pounds for specialist surgery, which involved almost completely reconstructing the leg with a series of specially made metal plates. John reckoned that the only time you could tell the leg was false was when Tigger was moving just a shade too fast and accidentally "clanged" against a hard surface.

Rebuilt to last –
Tigger on display
after his operation.

Purdey the cat probably owes her life to another animal – her best friend, Max the labrador. When out hunting in the Berkshire village of Woodley, Purdey took one leap too far and impaled herself on a two-foot-long iron spike which someone had carelessly left lying around. The poor cat struggled home dragging the spike with her, and somehow made it through the cat-flap before

28

collapsing beside Max's basket. By the time their owner, Karen Edwards, came down for breakfast, Max had licked the horrific wounds clean. "We could tell by the way her fur was wet that he had looked after her," said Karen, whisking Purdey off to the vet to ensure a full recovery.

Owner Kathleen Oates kept covering Flo with margarine in the hope that she would lick it off.

They thought time was running out for an elderly tortoiseshell called Flo when all her fur started dropping out. That was until a vet in the Lancashire

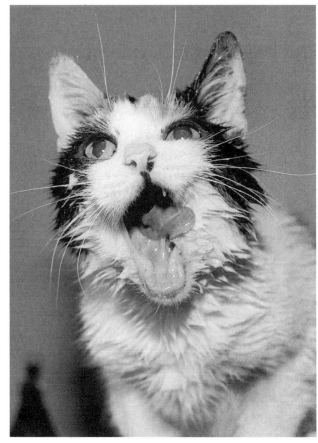

Flo, the cat that got the margarine.

town of Rossendale prescribed what he called "a fat treatment". Carefully obeying instructions, owner Kathleen Oates kept covering Flo with margarine in the hope that she would lick it off. The unorthodox cure worked. Flo developed a shiny new coat, and went back to being her old playful self. It was obviously quite a shock to the system – but nothing like the shock experienced by Sedgwick, a black and white cat that blacked out most of Cambridge for several hours by being a touch too adventurous with an electricity transformer. He walked straight into thirty-three thousand volts – and survived. His owner found him wandering around dazed, nursing severe burns and a leg injury. There was general

He walked straight into thirty-three thousand volts – and survived.

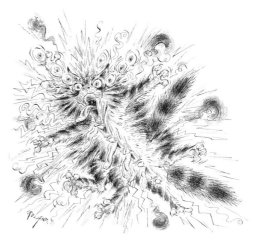

agreement that he had used up all of his nine lives in one go.

As indeed did Blackie, a fourteen-year-old tom whose story helped lift morale during the Second World War. He was warming himself in his favourite corner of the sitting-room hearth at home in Surbiton, when the German Air Force delivered a bomb down the chimney. His owner – an actress described simply as Miss L.Darlisle (undue familiarity was frowned upon in those days) – thought he had been killed, as half her house disappeared in rubble. Three days later, a hungry Blackie struggled out of the ruins, the only battle scar being the loss of one ear.

Another tomcat – unnamed, presumably to preserve his pride – was lucky not to lose rather more than an ear when he got trapped in the fanbelt of a car. He'd crept under the bonnet during the night, and clearly panicked in the confined space when the driver came out and tried to start his car in the morning. Goodness knows what the fanbelt did to him, but the kind of experience more in keeping with a Tom and Jerry cartoon horrified the driver when he finally got round to opening the bonnet of his old Volvo. The Bath fire brigade were called, and, doing their best to preserve as much as possible of both cat and car, took two hours to free the terrified animal. "It was completely disoriented," commented a brigade spokesman, "but otherwise none the worse for wear."

Blackie, the dog-eared cat.

30

CATSKILLS

What does your cat do if you place it in front of a mirror? Does it (**a**) look up, down, everywhere but at the mirror; (**b**) show interest in its reflection; (**c**) attempt to scratch the reflection; or (**d**) look behind the mirror for another cat? If the answer is (**d**), you have a really smart cat on your hands.

If the answer is (d), you have a really smart cat on your hands.

That is just one of the special tests devised by New York academic Peter Mandel to help owners measure their cats' IQ. His four-page questionnaire, rating cats by their responses to a series of everyday feline situations, went on sale for two dollars in the growing number of American shops devoted exclusively to pussy paraphernalia. Mr Mandel confessed that he was fully expecting irate customers to say it was a cheap piece of junk and demand their money back – but instead the response turned out to be overwhelming.

The British Cat Protection League took a more reserved view. It's director, George Stiller, cautiously admitted that "different species of animals do display different types of intelligence". But he appeared to disagree with Mr Mandel's controversial assertion that long-haired cats are cleverer than those with short hair. In Mr Stiller's opinion it was all down to the experience of life: "The more cats rely upon their instincts, the more they develop them, so a streetwise moggy could be smarter than a cossetted throroughbred. There has," he confessed, "been work carried out on cat intelligence in Britain, but I am not sure that one can actually measure it." So it was left to the Sunday Express to whet the British appetite for Mr Mandel's IQ test, in April 1990, by publishing a few more sample questions :

Place your cat inside a pet carrier. He (**a**) remains passive; (**b**) scratches and cries; (**c**) works to unfasten the door or lock; (**d**) successfully escapes.

At feeding time does your cat respond to the sound of: (**a**) food being scraped into a dish; (**b**) a can-opener or food box; (**c**) you calling 'dinner'; (**d**) you approaching the feeding area.

Your cat's favourite hiding place is: (**a**) in an open box; (**b**) under the kitchen table; (**c**) in a cupboard; or (**d**) you've never found the place.

In order to wake you up, your cat: (**a**) miaows quietly; (**b**) knocks things over; (**c**) sits on your head or chest; or (**d**)starts the coffee brewing.

As before, Mr Mandel insists that for the cleverest cats, (**d**) is the correct answer.

So, before you develop too great an inferiority complex on behalf of your

Three times a day she sneaked into the bar to help herself to a packet of pork scratchings.

pet, let me show you what can be achieved by cats of quite average brain. If, as many suspect, food is the prime motivator, then

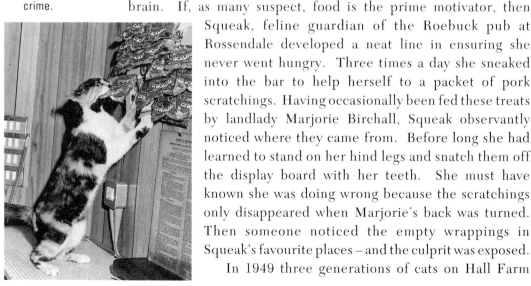

Squeak owns up and recreates the crime.

Squeak, feline guardian of the Roebuck pub at Rossendale developed a neat line in ensuring she never went hungry. Three times a day she sneaked into the bar to help herself to a packet of pork scratchings. Having occasionally been fed these treats by landlady Marjorie Birchall, Squeak observantly noticed where they came from. Before long she had learned to stand on her hind legs and snatch them off the display board with her teeth. She must have known she was doing wrong because the scratchings only disappeared when Marjorie's back was turned. Then someone noticed the empty wrappings in Squeak's favourite places – and the culprit was exposed.

In 1949 three generations of cats on Hall Farm

near Chesterfield found a way of ensuring the direct transfer of milk from cow to customer. It was Judy who discovered it first. She turned up at milking time, and miaowed so long and hard that Farmer Richardson – just to keep her quiet – squirted some milk into her mouth. Judy not only came back for more, but passed the word on to her daughter Susie who in turn taught the trick to her daughter, Tibby. Soon all three were forming a not-so-orderly queue every milking time.

Above

Not impressed – Kitty retrieves a wayward throw.

Above left

Milk straight from the cow for Judy and her family.

The clever cat took to retrieving the darts with her paws and sliding them down the board.

Two customers were playing darts in the bar of the Black Swan Hotel, Newcastle-upon-Tyne in 1939 when a young stray cat wandered in. It watched three arrows speed to their targets, then jumped up, took them out of the board and carried them back to one of the players. Before long, Kitty had been accepted as a member of the team – trusting some players enough to stand on the safety table the whole time their darts were whizzing past. The learning curve was sharp – the clever cat took to retrieving the darts with her paws and sliding them down the board so they didn't stick into her. It was another twenty-four years before a kitten with similar abilities turned up – this time to delight the darts players who worked in the Melting House of the Royal Mint.

Yuri Kouklachev provided the star attraction of the Moscow State Circus's 1985 European tour. He taught cats to play chess. Overcoming the legendary independence of Siamese, Siberian, Persian and plain stray cats, he trained them with infinite patience and care. "I noticed that cats were more alive at night," he explained. "So I began to play with them at night. I gained their confidence and began to teach them simple tricks." It wasn't easy. One of the acts took three years to perfect.

He also had the power to heal illness and injury in humans.

No training appears to have been necessary for Gus (Fergus) Bailey of Lyme Regis. *She* magazine reported in 1989 that the six-month-old ginger tom not only retrieved crumpled bits of paper like a dog, but he also had the power to heal illness and injury in humans. According to his owner, Jane Bailey, he inherited these powers from her first star pet, Rogan, whom people still talk about with awe in that corner of the West Country. "A woman needed help for the back problem spondylitis. So Jane held Gus against the woman's spine, and he knew where to apply his paws, walking up and down locating pain. The following day the woman went swimming in the hotel pool." Another lady, Phyllis Cox, had seen Rogan's name in the local press, and came to consult him about her osteoarthritis. Her daughter Bridget drove to Jane's home, and the four of them went off to the church where Rogan liked his "laying on of paws" to take place. "Once inside an odd thing happened. Rogan went to Bridget, the daughter, who hadn't asked for help. It was strange", recalled Jane. "Rogan insisted on sitting on Bridget, hissing and spitting, and then he seemed to react to something and jumped off. His diagnostic powers had detected a riding injury, and he'd sat with Bridget until he'd felt things were all right – then he moved to Mrs Cox. So successful was the treatment, Mrs Cox's consultant actually recommended she return to Rogan for a second session." It was further explained that Rogan's fur was combed out daily, and the strands, which had "remarkable" properties were parcelled up by Jane to send to people who needed help. "One woman wrote asking for help in treating the nervous shock she was suffering since being mugged. I sent her a hank of Rogan's fur, which she carried about with her. As she recovered, the fur changed into a hard ball. When she felt able to go out without it, she left it on her dressing table. After a few days she noticed it had begun growing again, and seemed to be surrounded by a luminous aura, a sort of glowing halo." At one stage, ninety people a week were said to be seeking Rogan's help. To those who – to put it mildly – find this all hard to believe, Jane had an answer. "Of course people think I'm mad. But I think he appeared as a cat to avoid the money and greed attached to humans."

After that, talking cats will come as something of a relief! In 1968, tourists with tape recorders were reported to be flocking to a house in the Turkish town of Konya to meet Pala, a five-year-old black and white tom cat that had built up quite a vocabulary. According to businessman Eyup Mutluturk and his wife, their pet began talking when he became jealous of one of their baby grandchildren. The words he spoke – in Turkish, of course – were mother, father, sister and Kamile (which was Mrs Mutluturk's first name). Konya's chief vet confirmed that Pala spoke like a one-year-old baby. Scientists were said to be interested in him too, but there is, as yet, no sign of an academic course on "How To Teach Your Cat to Talk".

Some years later, a bright spark in the Italian seaside town of Camogli tried to make a lira or two by putting Chicchiri, the talking cat, up for auction. Associated Press reported that the cat sat in total silence while not a single bidder offered the reserve price of

Pillion-passenger Maurice, out for a spin.

£67 ($160). The slump in Chicchiri's value was apparently caused by her failure to talk in front of television cameras.

The year-old tomcat would miaow piteously and rub up against his owner's leg until he was allowed to ride pillion.

Whenever cashier Roger Bullen went out on his motorbike in the Essex town of Chingford, his cat Maurice insisted on coming along too. The year-old tomcat would miaow piteously and rub up against his owner's leg until he was allowed to ride pillion. Quite at ease on shopping or sightseeing trips, Maurice only got upset if Mr Bullen took the bike's speed above thirty-five miles an hour. Sharp claws in his back signalled the cat's displeasure – and perhaps his concern that he might be blown off. All this was before the introduction of regulations requiring motorcycle passengers to wear helmets. Even so, the law found a reason to stop Maurice's fun. One day, as the duo were returning from a trip to a tea stall in Epping Forest, where the cat had enjoyed a saucer of milk, they were flagged down by a

One of the staff showed her to the elevator and pushed the button for the fourth floor.

policeman. Some months later, Mr Bullen was fined twenty pounds with five pounds costs for carrying Maurice in a way likely to cause him injury or unnecessary suffering. Maurice was unavailable to give evidence in his master's defence. Banished from his favourite pastime, he had run away a few weeks before.

Every morning, Mauki, the grey tabby, would walk down the sixty steps from the Stock family's fourth-floor apartment to go hunting. And every evening she would walk back up again – until someone gave her a ride in the lift. From then on, whenever she was ready to come in for the night she sauntered into the foyer and sat lazily on the reception desk until one of the staff showed her to the elevator and pushed the button for the fourth floor. While going up in the world, Mauki avoided climbing more than sixty-five thousand steps.

Tibs the tomcat made such a mess of the front door with his scratching to be let in that his owner, Harold Rogers of Dorchester in Oxfordshire, fixed a special door bell for him to ring. It was one of those sensitive instruments that ring at the slightest touch – and, over the following six months, Mr Rogers and his wife Mary hardly got a single good night's sleep. Tibs quickly realised he was on to a good thing – and, instead of coming home at his usual time of ten o'clock, stayed out later and later with his girlfriends. Then he just rang and rang until he was let in. Said seventy-three-year-old Mr Rogers: "He thinks he can come back any old time now. Often he's got us up at three or four in the morning." The

Tibs abusing the system.

answer? A ten o'clock curfew – and if Tibs was not in by then, the bell was disconnected. And to hell with the scratches on the front door.

Florence Swann of Thetford had a special cat, Timothy, who saw it all from the other side. Florence was deaf. So Timothy acted as her ears, and told her whenever there was someone ringing

While some may have been impressed with Malta's cup-holding cat, Smoky from Leicester preferred his tipple in a glass, with a drop of water.

the doorbell. "He really was clever," she said. "He used to come and hit me with his paw because he knew I couldn't hear." After all – it could have been Tibs trying another door after his 10pm curfew!

In 1965 a cat called Pussy, owned by Miss Salvina Cutajar, became one of Malta's star attractions because of its ability to drink from a cup or mug – which it gripped between its paws and lifted to its mouth. There was no posing or trickery in the photographs of the cat in action, eagerly seized upon by the world's press. Pussy performed on cue for television and films too. No-one taught her to do it – but she proved unable to pass on the trick to her offspring, who made it plain they preferred the more traditional saucer.

American Faye Murrell put in five or six hours every single day for a year training her cat, Shandy, to give up eating food directly off a saucer in favour of a fork and spoon, or chopsticks. She started as soon as he was weaned. Standing on a chair, his left front paw on the table, he's only too happy to have a fork or chopsticks attached to his right paw so he can use them to scoop up his food. After demonstrating his technique on the famous Hollywood programme *Astonishing Animals*, offers for advertising and TV shows poured in. Shandy was definitely one up on the cat – recalled by an animal expert in *Woman* magazine – who couldn't be bothered to get up to eat, and reached out from his basket to scoop food from a saucer with one stately paw!

Shandy, dressed for dinner.

Just to complete this round-up of domestic feline habits, there has to be a cat that has taught himself to use the family loo. There is! Louis, a sixteen-year-old Brown Burmese who lives in Torquay is the most house-trained cat in Britain. His owner, Joan Kilby, who was sixty-eight when the story hit the headlines, described in detail how he did it. "He sits on the seat, takes aim down the pan, and in a tinkle he's finished. And", she went on, "it's time he learned to flush the loo! He opens the door himself, so he should be able to master that too. But", she confided hastily, "it's only for Number One. For anything else he goes outside."

"He sits on the seat, takes aim down the pan, and in a tinkle he's finished."

A few cats have been known to provide a different kind of tinkle – on the piano. In 1989, police were called to the post office in Glanvilles Wootton, near Sherborne in Dorset, after residents heard the piano being played in the night. They found that the "intruder" was the pet cat. And Henry Stanhope, in *The Times*, recalled his Aunt's cat, Smuts, a piano player of some note, who "pussyfooted in C sharp" to draw attention to his plight. It all began when he started spending his afternoons in

In 1883 the French magazine *La Nature* proposed a use for cats with a musical inclination.

Arming herself with a poker, my aunt grimly advanced upon the sitting room.

the sitting room, "floating in a pool of sunlight, purring in his dreams and gently hiccupping after a good lunch. The risk he ran was that some passing member of the household, on seeing the sitting room door ajar, would promptly shut it. When Smuts wearied of his sybaritic lifestyle...he found his exit firmly blocked. As the kitchen was at the back of the house, down a long hallway, there was no-one to hear his disgruntled miaowing. One day, acting, probably, more out of frustration than according to any preconceived plan, he leaped on to the piano and ran in exasperation up and down the keyboard. The result sounded like Stockhausen on a good day. Now the sound of someone playing the piano, however badly, in an otherwise empty house, is enough to cause instant alarm. Arming herself with a poker and accompanied by other members of the family, my aunt grimly advanced upon the sitting room. In some fear and trepidation they flung open the door, upon which Smuts sprang down from his rostrum and, tail high in the air like a token of complaint, stalked sulkily out of the room." But that wasn't the end of it. Smuts warmed to the attention his new talents commanded. Henry

PLAY IT AGAIN, SMUTS

Stanhope warmed to his theme: "This Pussini of the pianoforte, this Chatkovsky of the keyboard began to perform not only as a means of communications but out of a clear desire to entertain. While his proud owner and friends stood by and applauded, he slithered over the ivories on velvet paws, purring in satisfaction to earn himself tinned sock-eye salmon for tea...sometimes, when the wind is blowing from the Styperstones and the Shropshire plain is slumbering in the sun, I fancy I can hear Smuts playing on – another little sound on earth from Heaven".

IN NEED OF A HOME

"Have put to sleep - gone on holiday." That was the heart-rending message attached to a sack dumped on the doorstep of an Edmonton housewife in 1958. Inside were two kittens, who, it turned out, were anything but asleep. And fifty-six-year-old Mrs Cissie Walledge had no hesitation in coming quickly to the rescue. She took them in, plied the starving creatures with food, and set about finding them a new home.

Eleven years later and it was Ruffles "the orphan kitten", as one writer plaintively described him, who peered sad and bewildered out of the morning's newspapers, alongside the carrier bag in which his owner had abandoned him at Sutton in Surrey. The RSPCA promised to find a home for him. After such wide publicity there was no shortage of offers.

Then there was Sooty, "the kitten nobody wanted", rescued from the River Thames with half a brick tied around his neck. A few days of tender loving care later, the nation was treated to the sequel - Sooty's remarkable transformation into a kitten fit to grace the cover of a chocolate box.

Discarded kittens: the two found in a sack by Mrs Walledge (top) and Ruffles, with his paper bag.

Then there was Sooty, rescued from the River Thames with half a brick tied around his neck.

Such stories are all too common, making the tabloid pages of a cat-loving nation with a frequency which owes not a little to the heartfelt desire to sell more newspapers. They also graphically remind us of the lengths to which some people will go to dispose of unwanted

 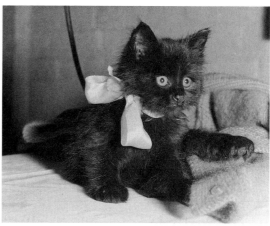

Sooty, saved from the river, and (right) the happy ending.

kittens - and the combination of spontaneous warmth and outrage which motivates others to save them. They also highlight the remarkable capacity of some cats to survive the worst that the human world can throw at them.

Jill Mantell reckons she has seen - and revived - just about every kind of mistreated cat. Known as the "Cat Lady" in her native East End of London, she rescues - and finds homes for - around a thousand cats a year, and can have as many as forty of them in her house at any one time. Her vet's bill runs to twenty pounds a week - with another ten pounds for cat litter, and fifty pounds more for food.

Her vet's bill runs to twenty pounds a week – with another ten pounds for cat litter, and fifty pounds more for food.

And what food! Every morning she opens ten large tins of tasty cat morsels, and every evening she cuts up and cooks ten pounds of meat. Jill even goes to the trouble of mincing some of the meat "for those cats who have no teeth because they've had gum disease". There's specially enriched milk for those who turn up thin and starving; an appropriate milk substitute for motherless kittens; and extra vitamins for all and sundry. And just to complete this cats' utopia, new arrivals are

treated to a de-fleaing spray and then a hot-water bottle in a cosy basket next to Jill's bed.

There is no shortage of would-be new owners promising to give these cats more of the good life they clearly missed in earlier days - but one moggy had his nerves so shattered by a truly appalling experience that Jill decided any move would be too traumatic. So Pickles is the only cat that stays permanently with her. Someone had forced a jam jar over his head, and left him to suffocate. This clever cat banged the jar against a wall or pavement until it broke. He could breathe again, but was left with a jagged glass collar which cut into his neck and which he had no means of removing. When Jill found him, the sharp edges of the glass had cut away some of his fur, and parts of his neck were bald. It didn't

Someone had forced a jam jar over his head, and left him to suffocate.

take long to get Pickles back into good shape, but his continuing nervousness is a permanent reminder of what he went through.

Jill ties down a full-time job as receptionist for the local council, but every spare moment, evenings and weekends, is spent caring for her tribe of cats - or out hunting for new recruits to swell their ranks. "I often have to climb through derelict blocks of flats in pursuit of an injured cat," she said. "I lure them with food so I can get a proper look at them and see what the problem is. Families are uprooted in re-housing schemes and they just abandon their pets, leaving them to roam the streets. People often can't afford, or can't be bothered, to have their cats neutered, so a female will have litter after litter."

"It's emotional blackmail, but I can't say no. I'll never let a cat die."

News of Jill's all-consuming interest in cats spread quickly through the East End, with many people rounding up animals for her, but others taking advantage of her concern in a quite shameful way. "I've had people threaten to flush kittens down the loo if I don't take the litter away from them. I even had one man threaten to electrocute his mother cat and kittens. It's emotional blackmail, but I can't say no. I'll never let a cat die."

The children who brought Bedknobs to her knew that. The owners of this three-month-old kitten had put him in a plastic bag, sealed it - presumably in the hope that he would suffocate - and just left the bag hanging on some park railings. The children saw the bag moving and called in Jill to guarantee a happy ending.

Joan Beech with Magique, the cat which prompted a rescue mission in Kenya.

Some people go much further afield for their cat rescues. In Kenya during the 1950s, the Mau Mau waged a campaign of terror against white settlers in their fight for independence. Their symbol was a crucified cat! Song-writer Joan Beech found one crouching against a wall on the brink of death. His legs were tied with knotted string, and his front paws were broken. It took Joan six weeks to nurse him back to health. Then she and a friend, Nan Coton, rounded up others threatened with a similar fate at the hands of the Mau Mau, and brought them back to Britain on their plane.

It's not only humans who rescue cats. Sometimes other animals help out as well. Everyone thought that Lucky the kitten had drowned when the car in which he was travelling came off the road and somersaulted into a water-filled culvert. The car was lifted out and removed to a scrap yard at Llantrisant in South Wales. It was about to be crunched into a two-foot-wide block of metal in a giant

compressing machine when the yard's guard dog – a Great Dane called Bosley – started nosing about. He smelled cat! Attracted by his barking, the yard's owner found Lucky trapped and miaowing under the front passenger seat. The cat that really lived up to his name quickly found a new home with nine-year-old Gemma Callow.

A restraining hand holds Bosley who seems keen to claim "finders – keepers".

Occasionally you'll find cats prepared to take matters into their own hands. One called Kim even wrote for help to the *Daily Mirror*'s famous agony aunt, Marjorie Proops. His letter - penned, of course, with just a little help from a neighbour - tugged at several hundred heart-strings. "Dear Marje," he wrote, "my mistress has been in hospital for six months; I have missed her terribly, but there is no sign of her coming back, and now it

"I am spayed, slightly nervous and don't really like dogs."

appears I am about to be evicted from our flat. I am spayed, slightly nervous and don't really like dogs. Can anyone offer me a new home?" From the avalanche of replies, Kim picked out fourteen-year-old Isobel Sneddon from Dulwich in South London, who promised the lonely cat "lots of kisses and cuddles".

Perhaps an even cleverer tactic was adopted by the cat who wandered onto the set of the soap opera *Dynasty* with a sign around his neck saying "Please Give Me a Home". Production stopped while stars John Forsythe, Linda Evans, Joan Collins and Stephanie Beecham all claimed the cat. The argument was resolved by drawing straws - and the cat settled down to a comfortable life with John Forsythe.

Cats who hit the headlines are seldom short of offers of a new home. One exception was Wilfred, whose battle scars and double chin earned him the nickname of the ugliest cat in the country. Try as they might, the Torquay branch of the RSPCA could find no-one to take him in - until the Glover family came along to prove that there's an owner somewhere for even the unlikeliest of cats.

Ownership of one lost stray was claimed by forty different people after his escapade made national television. Sammy - later nicknamed Lofty for *obvious* reasons - caused chaos by climbing a 150-foot chimney at Bolton in Lancashire just as workmen were preparing to demolish it. This proved to be one

problem too far for the RSPCA - and the fire brigade's ladder turned out to be just too short. It was clearly a case for veteran steeplejack Fred Dibnah, who tried every trick in the book to lure or cajole the scared moggy into his arms. The nationwide television news coverage of this epic struggle between man and cat went on for the best part of two days, drawing a considerable crowd. Instead of Fred, it was one of the onlookers who brought the drama to an end. Gerry Rogers, a factory worker from Manchester and member of a group called Animals in Distress, waited until the steeplejack nipped off for a meal break, and quickly shinned up his ladder before anyone could stop him. He quickly coaxed Lofty towards him, grabbed the cat by the scruff of the neck, and gingerly made a one-handed descent. Safely at the bottom, he walked into a round of applause - and the police! "They told me I was an idiot," said Gerry, "but promised I wouldn't be charged with anything." And Fred, back from his lunch, neatly mixed his own annoyance with genuine admiration - "He was fool, but I admire his bravery." After all that, Lofty was famous - and had to fight off the queue of people claiming to be his owner. By a process that no-one could quite explain, it was eventually whittled down to two-year-old Daniel Gudjoc, clearly delighted to have his pet back after such a hair-raising adventure.

Joseph, a two-stone tabby cat, ended up with more than the usual home comforts. He had a bank account as well!

Joseph, a two-stone tabby cat, ended up with more than the usual home comforts. He had a bank account as well! His owner, spinster Agatha Higgins, of Petersham in Surrey, left him £369 in her will, published in November 1969. With the cash came instructions to her housekeeper to spend it at the rate of one pound a week to keep Joseph in food for the rest of his life. At 1969 prices, that added up to more than enough of his favourite fish, cream and rabbit steaks to ensure the portly Joseph kept his personal pot right up to the very end.

CATS AND THE LAW

Cats may well be laws unto themselves, but no cat is above the law of the land - nor, for that matter, are its owners. Tax inspectors conducted a "purge" of West Country farmers in 1988, after discovering that some were offsetting the cost of food for farmyard cats against their tax bills. What the Inland Revenue called "exotic cats being run on the business" came in for particular attention. After long consultations, the Farmers' Union grimly informed its members that "Siamese or Persian cats cannot be claimed for as farm mousers - and that's official!" No evidence for the defence was offered on behalf of the felines in question, who were probably too upset at the shameful implication that they had forsaken hunting around the farmyard in favour of

"Siamese or Persian cats cannot be claimed for as farm mousers – and that's official!"

lazy spoonfuls from a tin.

But even padding around farms is not as innocent and trouble-free a past-time as cats might think. It landed one German tabby in the middle of a lawsuit. Chased by a dog, she ran into a stable where a cow was being milked, and took refuge on the animal's back. Not surprisingly, this frightened the cow, which kicked the milkmaid off her stool. The milkmaid proceeded to sue the owner of the cat, Captain Bangel, the owner of the dog, Herr Schmidt, *and* the owner of the cow, Herr Kameler. After lengthy arguments, the court awarded the milkmaid the princely sum of twelve pounds, with the rather more substantial costs being split evenly between the three defendants.

Captain Bangel's cat, unconcerned at all the fuss.

While some cats simply cause trouble, one actually caused a crime wave - and he wasn't even real. Garfield, the fat cat with the drooping eyelids and a lust for lasagne, was created by cartoonist Jim Davis in 1977. Within five years his strip was appearing in 450 newspapers and the first of many best-selling paperbacks was on sale. His popularity bred demands for all kinds of Garfield products, but it wasn't until the marketing men began targeting motorists that the orange-striped cat became - if you'll pardon the phrase - a catalyst for crime. A ten-inch tall, cuddly Garfield was produced, with suction pads on his paws so he could be attached to car windows. Drivers in their thousands

Garfield, trapped inside a Ford Escort, appeals for release.

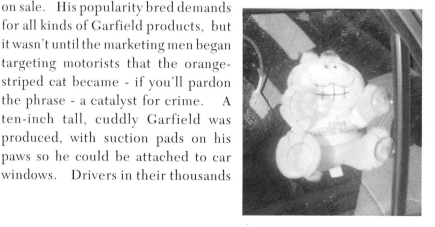

forked out seventeen pounds a time for this latest status symbol, and before long a new breed of car thief was in action. Throughout London and the South-East of England police reported hundreds of car windscreens smashed for the sole purpose of "liberating" Garfield. And the usual targets of car radios and stereos remained, in most cases, untouched.

Cat-loving motorists faced a real-life dilemma in 1985 when the German Institut für Demoskopie, Allensbach sought their reaction to a case which split the legal profession. A driver had caused an accident by braking

Police reported hundreds of car windscreens smashed for the sole purpose of "liberating" Garfield.

suddenly to avoid a cat. As a result, a driver following behind hit his car. The first court to hear the case fined the first driver because "he put on his brakes without sufficient cause". But, on appeal, a higher court lifted the sentence on the grounds that "someone who likes cats has sufficient reason to brake". The poll turned into a duel between love of car and love of cat. Overall, 47 per cent of those questioned agreed with the final verdict, 36 per cent did not, while 17 per cent were undecided. Among the women, the cat-lovers had an even bigger majority - 53 per cent to 30 per cent. But men narrowly backed the orginal verdict by 43 per cent to 40 per cent, and a British court would probably have agreed with that, arguing that the motorist who hits you from behind is usually to blame on the grounds that if he can't brake in time he is almost certainly driving too close.

A Virginia judge had absolutely no doubts about the eight-month jail sentence he imposed on 28-year-old Michael Stoner, who arrived home drunk one evening in the town of Roanoke, Virginia, shot a neighbour's cat, and then drove over it with his car to try to make the death look accidental. At one point, General District Judge James Brice was so upset he offered to disqualify himself from the case because he had owned cats most of his life, even had one with the same name as the dead pet - Samantha - and found himself in sympathy with the owner. Stoner, who said he'd no objection to the judge, claimed he'd shot the cat because a friend told him it was a stray who'd been causing trouble. It was only after the shooting, when he heard it was a neighbour's cat, that he decided to make it look like an accident by running over it with his car. Stoner would have got a full year in prison if he hadn't agreed to compensate the owner for veterinary bills. Rather luckier were two Cumbrian women who were give a twelve-month conditional discharge when accused of causing criminal damage to a cat. Sally Steele and Louise Simpson were fed up with being woken at night by the noisy, romantic exploits of Fudge the tomcat, who, they said, had also entered their homes to "mark territory". So they kidnapped him and took him to a vet to be neutered. The fur really flew when his owner, Maureen Hogg, found out - and the two ladies were hauled before the Whitehaven magistrates where they confessed to their "crime".

Two more neighbours went to law in Passau, West Germany, over an allegation that Bubu, a tomcat, was straying into the next-door garden and soiling it. The judge upheld the complaint, and ordered Bubu's owners - Elizabeth and Franz Baier - to keep their

Bubu, the tomcat who didn't wander far enough.

cat locked up inside their home or pay a fine of $200,000. The ruling incensed West German cat-lovers, who campaigned in vain to have it reversed.

More usually, what leads a cat to court is a characteristic combination of its cunning and its appetite - in short, its tendency to call in at several houses in a neighbourhood every day in the hope of collecting a meal at each. Not unnaturally, most people feed a cat if they think they own it. When two mottled grey cats turned up at the home of Leeds United centre-forward John Pearson, his wife Tina - thinking they were strays - offered them a saucer of milk and a plate of fish. Virgil and Poppy took to popping back for more, often staying the night, and giving the clear impression they had moved in. It was only after two years of these comings and goings, when the Pearsons moved to a new home a mile up the road, and took the cats with them, that neighbour Jane Gregory angrily declared the animals to be hers. *She* thought the cats had been spending their nights simply wandering the streets. She had, she said, proof of ownership, and would fight - through the courts if necessary - for their return. But Mrs Pearson felt confident. As well as feeding the cats every day, she said she'd paid vet's fees for annual vaccinations and even to have the male cat castrated. She had, she added, talked to a solicitor, the RSPCA and the Citizen's Advice Bureau, and all had advised her to keep the cats. Jane Gregory admitted that the onus was on her to prove ownership.

That was nothing compared to the achievement of Marmaduke Gingerbits, a tomcat who dragged battling neighbours in the Essex town of Woodford Bridge through a legal contest that lasted no fewer than nine months. On the one side were Police Constable John Sewell and his wife Anna, who said he belonged to them. On the other was Monty Cohen, who claimed the cat's real name was Sonny, and he was his. Marmaduke - or Sonny - didn't really mind. He spent most of the legal proceedings being cared for in police custody at a cost of £1.40 a day! The dispute ended up in Bow County Court where

Tina with Virgil and Poppy: 'They stay here,' she insists

Fur flies over soccer star's adopted cats

A CAT lover plans to go to court over two pets adoped by soccer star John Pearson and his wife.

They were taken in by Tina Pearson and the Leeds United centre forward after turning up at the couple's home two years ago.

Tina, thinking they were strays, gave them a dish of fish and a saucer of milk.

Virgil and Poppy gradually became regular visitors, often staying the night.

But neighbour Jane Gregory says the mottled grey cats are hers.

The issue has split the tiny village of Malin Bridge, near Sheffield.

Miss Gregory thought the cats were simply spending the nights wandering the streets.

Last week, however, they failed to turn up on her doorstep for breakfast after the Pearsons moved to a new home a mile away, taking "their" pets with them.

Miss Gregory, 25, said: "Mrs Pearson offered me £500 to buy them. But they are not for sale.

"I had no idea they were staying nights with the Pearsons. I have proof of ownership and I will fight for my cats' return."

Mrs Pearson, 27, said: "I've talked to a solicitor, the RSPCA and the Citizens' Advice Bureau. I've been advised by all of them to keep the cats.

"They have always slept in my house. I've given them meals every day. I paid for the vet to castrate the male cat and I've spent money on annual injections."

New home: Leeds star John

Jane: 'The cats are mine'

The cats appeared shortly after the couple moved into their previous home, said Tina.

She added: "We gave them titbits and they stayed.

"I would not have encouraged them. As far as I was concerned, no-one else was bothered. No-one ever challenged us about castrating the cat."

Jane said: "I suspected someone had been feeding them but did not know until last Wednesday who it was.

"Now it seems the onus is on me to prove ownership."

the Sewells clinched their case with the claim that Marmaduke had an allergy to milk, and summoned to the witness box an RSPCA inspector who testified that this was indeed so. There was some small consolation for the loser when the court found that Constable Sewell had been wrong to "put an armlock on Mr Cohen", and ordered the Sewells to pay him £50 for "assault and trespass" and £200 of his costs. As for Marmaduke Gingerbits, he was given star media treatment. He was rushed past waiting photographers with a blanket over his basket, and whisked away in a fast car. He was, it seems, accompanied by a representative of a national newspaper which had bought up his "exclusive" story - the claws were out in tabloid territory once again!

Derby's Weights and Measures Department was called into action when a woman complained that a shopkeeper had sold her a female kitten when she'd asked for a tom. The department's view - that this was an infringement of the Trades Descriptions Act - was upheld in court, and the shopkeeper and her aggrieved customer agreed to share the cost of an operation on the cat to prevent it having a litter.

One summer the government passed a law banning cats (and dogs) from swimming off the country's beaches.

One of the most bizarre cat cases surfaced at Croydon County Court, when Else Athaide complained that a taxidermist had turned her beloved deceased cat Mimi into "a cross-eyed monster". An expert confirmed that "the eyes did indeed face opposite directions". A distressed Mrs Athaide said it had been "just terrible" - an experience that won her £361 compensation.

Few countries have specific laws governing the behaviour of cats or their owners. Greece is an exception. One summer the government passed a law banning cats (and dogs) from swimming off the country's beaches. It made owners liable to a fine of £300 if their pets infringed public health regulations by taking a dip. Hardly a mighty revenue earner - but it could just explain the phrase "cool cats".

SMALL SCREEN CATS

The year was 1956, ITV had just arrived, and a more adventurous world was opening up in television. There was new ground to be broken, and cats were ready to play their part amongst the new pioneers. Possibly the most controversial programme of that year (which is some measure of how they rated controversies in those days!) starred a heavily pregnant Trixie, poised to produce her four kittens during a children's TV programme. It was the idea of Mr Stuart Gelder of the Blue Cross Society, who arranged for a twenty-four-hour watch to be kept on Trixie. At the first signs of labour, a film unit would be summoned to record every detail - Trixie making a home, the first kitten emerging, Trixie licking her clean, the first feed, and so on. Mr Gelder wanted to teach children the reverence of life, and to do that, when the birth was over, he opened up the back of a watch to show its intricate mechanism. That, he said, was an example of the creative ability of man which no-one would want to destroy - yet the much more wonderful mechanism of the cat was destroyed thousands of times a year as unwanted kittens were disposed of.

Yet the much more wonderful mechanism of the cat was destroyed thousands of times a year as unwanted kittens were disposed of.

One of the first cats to appear in an advertisement on British television was Bonavia Campanello (sensibly nicknamed Susie), a Chinchilla kitten enlisted to extol the virtues of a particular type of carpet. Blazing a trail subsequently followed by many a star of TV advertising, Susie went on to appear in films such as *The Spaniards' Curse*

Doolish the tail-less travel executive

and *Orders To Kill*, where, needless to say, she had rather less of a starring role. Positively her last professional appearance (in Britain at least) was in the arms of Bristol cadet Robert Bisacre as she boarded the good ship MV *Port Phillip* in London's Royal Albert Dock, en route to a Miss R. Lovejoy of Palmerston North, New Zealand, who purchased the famous lady for an undisclosed sum.

Doolish, the executive cat, never made it to television. His more down-to-earth job was promoting holidays in the Isle of Man to the people of South-East England. His name was Manx for Douglas, the island's capital, and he was, not surprisingly, a tail-less Manx cat. As befitted his lengthy pedigree, he travelled to London in considerable style - first an executive cabin all of his own on the Isle of Man's Steam Packet Company Ferry, and then by train and taxi to the plush Mayfair offices that were to be his new home. The Manx Information Centre, clearly working on a tight budget, carefully costed his anticipated consumption of milk and tinned cat food, allowing just a little for inflation - and the expected inflation of the growing Doolish's appetite.

When the freshener was removed, Purr promptly knocked off his blindfold and tucked into the fish.

At least Doolish could see what he was doing - not so a cat called Purr, who appeared in a British-made commercial for Spanish television. In the advertisement, which was promoting an air freshener, Purr was blindfolded, and appeared unable to sniff out a succulent dish of fish because the tempting smell was blocked by this new,

Purr, the international award-winning advertiser.

powerful freshener. When the freshener was removed, Purr promptly knocked off his blindfold and tucked into the fish. Purr, owned by pet trainer Olive Tate from Bexleyheath in Kent, was so convincing that he helped the advertisement win a top Gold Award at the prestigious Venice Film Festival in 1983.

Tiddles, another of Olive Tate's animals, found TV stardom just over a year earlier, in a commercial in which the actor and comedian, John Cleese, decreed that a certain video recorder was "so simple that even a cat could operate it". Tiddles then appeared to push in the cassette and set the controls to start recording at ten-thirty. On this occasion, Olive, who took

Tiddles – deceptively lacking in technical skill.

three weeks to train the cat for the advertisement, revealed her secret. Tiddles had apparently been tempted by an old-fashioned "tickling stick", and simply "followed the feathers".

No such opportunity for Copper, a moggy from Portsmouth whose thirty seconds of advertising glory was thwarted by an owner who had no time at all for this television nonsense. A cat food company in Paris saw some amusing photographs of Copper "watching the birdie" through the viewfinder of a camera, and pushing a small pram full of his favourite meals. They thought he'd be pretty good at pushing their product as well, and crossed the Channel with fat contract in hand. But Copper's owner, Mrs Val Andrews, would have none of it - the promise of stardom paled into insignificance beside the thought of

John Cleese decreed that a certain video recorder was "so simple that even a cat could operate it".

her beloved cat having to spend six months in quarantine on the way back from his French filming assignment. "All right," said the determined Parisians, "we'll send a film production team to Britain." At that point, Mrs Andrews decided she was too busy looking after her two children to supervise her cat's screen début. "I'm sorry to spoil Copper's hour of glory," she said,"but we'll still love him, even if he isn't a TV star."

The RSPCA once tried to have a *toy* cat banned from a TV commercial. It was an advertisement for Prudential Assurance which showed the comedian Griff Rhys Jones throwing the toy through a window. The RSPCA said, "We know it is only a dummy cat, but even so it may encourage children to subject their cats to a similar ordeal - you never know. We don't have any power to force them off the air, but that is what we would wish them to do." The man from the Pru, advertising director Blackett Ditchburn, fought back, pointing out that "the research we did before the ad went out showed to our satisfaction that it would not offend. It is humorous, and wherever humour is involved, there will be those who like or dislike it. Besides", he added,"some thirty million people have seen this ad, and only 150 have complained." The Independent Broadcasting Authority had the final word, politely informing the RSPCA that the commercial conformed to its standards. Griff Rhys Jones and the mighty Pru both lived to advertise another day.

The only question mark over the next cat commercial was how on earth the film-makers had done it. It was one of the great love stories of 1988, commissioned by an organisation not easily associated with romance - The Solid Fuel Advisory Service. Charged with promoting coal fires, they called in the advertising agency Saatchi and Saatchi, who in turn enlisted the help of Sylvester the cat. But this was no solo role. The billing was to be shared with Matthew the bulldog and a very small white mouse called Mickey. To the sounds of the old pop hit "Will You Still Love Me Tomorrow",

Matthew strolled in and squatted happily in front of a blazing fire, followed by Sylvester, who kissed the dog and settled down beside him. Enter Mickey, fearlessly scurrying up to be rewarded, in turn, with yet another kiss. Adrian Kemsley and Charles Hendley, the admen who planned it, admitted that the kisses were simply a marvellous bonus - unexpected "sniffs" adlibbed by the curious (and no doubt amazed) Sylvester. The truth was that Sylvester only got his big break because the cat originally chosen for the part became so tensed up by these close encounters with his old enemies that he had to be dropped. And supercool Sylvester, the animal trainer's pet cat, just happened to be, as they say, in the right place at the right time - ready to step into stardom. Even so, he still had to be tempted by a few prawns hidden underneath the bulldog - prawns which, it must be said,

The famous friendly threesome.

He still had to be tempted by a few prawns hidden underneath the bulldog.

Millions of youngsters grew up adoring the cats that padded across the TV screens of their childhood.

Matthew quite fancied as well! And Mickey was not so much running towards the fire as running away from a technician's bright light. But there was universal agreement that the result was, in the words of the agency, "one of the most aaaaahhhhh advertisements ever made". What was it they used to say about never working with animals...?

Or, for that matter, with children. The BBC programme *Blue Peter* proved the old adage wrong on both counts, uniting animals and children with a magic formula of informality that has made it one of television's longest-running programmes. Millions of youngsters grew up adoring the cats that padded engagingly and unpredictably across the TV screens of their childhood. Cats like Jason, a seal point Siamese, who bestrode the programme for eleven years. The floods of national tears when he died were assuaged by the arrival of two three-week old silver tabbies. *Blue Peter*'s eight million viewers were asked to name them, and voted overwhelmingly for Jack and Jill.

The unnamed Blue Peter kittens make their first appearance, in the care of their mother and programme presenter Lesley Judd.

Others would follow in time, including Willow, a blue point Balinese variant - a long-haired Siamese born of a short-hair mother who carried a long-hair gene. The cats became stars in their own right, regularly touring the country for shows and personal appearances; but, above all, they have been invaluable in teaching children how to care for their own cats. For example, when Willow was neutered, the programme highlighted the need for pet cats to be spayed to prevent the problem of unwanted kittens. These top cats - and some of the other animals that appeared on the programme - were looked after by Edith Menezes, a well-known breeder and

Cruiser, retained by Universal Studios and much in demand for TV.

international judge, who became the longest-serving member of the *Blue Peter* team. Across three decades she brought the pets to the studio twice a week, and once revealed her tactics for making sure they did what the scripts demanded of them. "The cats are allowed to roam around the dressing room, and couldn't be more comfortable. When I know I've got half a minute, I put Willow on her cushion and "threaten" her - she's very inquisitive, you see, and won't always do as she's told, jumping down when you want her to stay. So I put cream cheese on her paws, and she sits there licking away at them as the credits roll."

Goodness knows what inducements were needed to persuade an American TV cat, Cruiser, to pose leisurely on a sunbed in the middle of a swimming pool. Or to train a cat named Dudley, who appeared on California's Channel Seven television during the late 1970s. He was said to perform no fewer than thirty separate tricks, including typing, playing checkers, rolling over and shaking hands.

This Greta Garbo of the cat world just arrived, as if on cue, for the filming, settled down for a snooze, and then vanished.

But some cats don't have to do very much to get themselves on television - they just happen to be around at the right time. Take, for example, the ginger moggy regularly seen sleeping on a rooftop during the opening titles of Britain's longest-running soap opera, *Coronation Street*. His identity remains a secret. This Greta Garbo of the cat world just arrived, as if on cue, for the filming, settled down for a snooze, and then vanished. But his slumbering image lingered on to invade the nation's living rooms repeatedly over fourteen years - until, in 1989, Granada decided the title sequence needed renewing. ITV's *This Morning* programme, ably assisted by Britain's tabloid press, led the search for a new cat. Applications poured in, and soon the producer's desk was littered with photographs of five thousand moggies. Ten were shortlisted, and *This Morning* filmed each of them in action, inviting viewers to select just five via a phone-in. That narrowed the competition down to Frisky from Leeds, Tiddles from Newcastle, Meechi from Manchester, Archie from Cheltenham and Teilo from Cardiff.

All of them were summoned to be screen-tested on the *Coronation Street* set. They were required to pad along a red carpet, nip into the Rovers Return, act a scene with Percy Sugden and Emily Bishop, get out of a Rolls Royce, negotiate a cat flap, walk down the Street and pose on a wall. Then they faced a panel of judges including Jean Alexander (who played Hilda Ogden) and comedian Ken Dodd. The decision was close, but the verdict unanimous - the new star of Coronation Street would be Frisky, a three-year-old tabby tom who looked the perfect, street-wise alley cat. It was only then that his owner, Mrs Joyce Rimington, confessed that he normally lived a life of luxury with five other cats in a converted castle just outside Leeds. The *Kennel and Cattery Management* magazine clearly overindulged itself in reporting the momentous decision. It speculated that the Rimingtons would "study in great detail every 'claws' in their moggy's contract, and sign an undertaking that Frisky would never, ever sell kiss-and-miaow stories to the tabby-loid press."

The need to place "small-screen" cats under close contract first surfaced twenty-one years earlier, when Arthur, the famous white cat who advertised pet food by eating it with his paw, found himself at the centre of a legal spat. A High Court judge was asked to decide whether Arthur belonged to the pet food manufacturers, Spillers, or to Mr Toneye Manning, a twenty-six-year-old actor. Spillers said they bought the cat from its original owner for £700. Mr Manning claimed he found Arthur in Hemel Hempstead in 1984, and, as he

"You can take it from me we are not interested in capitalist cats, no matter how much they earn as TV stars."

could not track down the owner, brought him to London. It was a case of high drama. The day of the first High Court hearing, the actor said Arthur was seeking political asylum in the Soviet embassy and had been handed over to a Russian diplomat. Such was the interest in the story that the Soviets briefly interrupted their Cold War wrangling with the United States to issue a formal denial. "We haven't seen your damned cat," wrote the Embassy Press Attaché, Mr Serge Rogov, "haven't offered it political asylum, and wouldn't want it about the place." Not one to miss an opportunity to score a political point, he added tersely, "You can take it from me we are not interested in capitalist cats, no matter how much they earn as TV stars."

Or, as the company's lawyer put it, "the grand total of Arthur plus £150,000".

Mr Manning was subsequently ordered to return Arthur to Spillers pending a full hearing of the case. When he failed to do so, he was imprisoned for fifteen days for contempt of court. The day after he started his jail sentence, Arthur was found in a cardboard box left on the doorstep of a television agent, Mr Terence D'Gray, and was duly handed over to Spillers. The case took almost another two years to wend its way back into the High Court, when Spillers demanded a declaration that Arthur belonged to them, and an injunction restraining Mr Manning from taking Arthur out of the country if he ever got hold of the cat again. The persistent Mr

The original Arthur helps to launch his biography.

Manning counterclaimed for the return of Arthur; personal damages of £60,000; £15,000 for witholding the cat illegally, and a further £75,000 for alleged false representation by Spillers. Or, as the company's lawyer put it, "the grand total of Arthur plus £150,000". Spillers won - and Arthur was able to relax even more into his starring TV role, working his usual nine days a year in front of the

cameras, and going on to adorn a range of T-shirts and towels and front a road safety campaign. He even had his life story published - *Arthur, the Television Cat*, ghosted by John Montgomery, and ended his sixteen years in comfortable retirement in a "sort of super cat hotel" in Essex.

Arthur's screen appearances would have cost more than thirty million pounds at today's rates - and, with that kind of pulling power, it was inevitable that a successor would have to be found. Ten years later, Anne Head was commissioned - in great secrecy - to find the new Arthur. Her search ended in Wood Green Animal Shelter in Hertfordshire, where staff were nursing a sickly white two-year-old stray back to health. "I picked him up and played with him for a few minutes," said Anne. "He looked ghastly, but I knew he was the right one." There was only one difference between the two Arthurs. Unlike the first one, lifting the food out of the tin with his paw didn't come naturally to Arthur number two - he had to be trained to do it.

Arthur No 2 practises his technique.

The Arthur saga - minus the litigation - had an almost precise parallel in America, where Morris was recruited to star in television commercials for one of the leading cat foods. His performance earned him a PATSY award in 1973, short for the Picture Animal Top Star of the Year Award, a sort of animal Oscar. He then entered the race for President of the United States, had his biography published, and when he died, his place was taken by Morris Two, also discovered in a cat's home.

IDENTITY CRISES

I t was perhaps inevitable that Morris the cat would become a candidate for the Presidency of the United States. After all, by 1988 he was already America's best known feline, appearing on prime-time television and touring the country for dozens of personal appearances. What clinched his decision to throw his hat into the ring for the White House was a national poll, revealing that he was better known than all the Republican and Democratic contenders, except George Bush. So, the 18th August found him calling a press conference at Washington's National Press Club to announce that he would run as an Independent, on a platform demanding equal rights for all felines and the millions of voters they represent.

So it was time for Morris – known as the Robert Redford of the cat world – to strike back.

In fact, the decision to take Morris into the world of politics could well have been a defensive decision. For nineteen years the splendid ginger tabby (and another looking remarkably like him) had been extolling the delights of Nine Lives, America's most popular cat food, in no fewer than eighty television commercials. He was a key factor in selling over a quarter of a million dollars worth of cat food a year. And he had watched other budding cat stars come and go as they peddled cars, airlines, telephones, banks, health insurance, business machines, diet drinks and sleeping pills. But now Morris's position as top cat was seriously threatened. A young upstart - a silver tabby called Tyrone - was knocking the viewers' socks off in a whole range of TV commercials. Already he had forty to his credit - and the Nippon Telegraph and Telephone Company had even sent a crew from Japan to film him in one of their

Morris on the campaign trail.

advertisements. What's more, he had dared to appear on two TV talk shows! So it was time for Morris - known as the Robert Redford of the cat world - to strike back. And even if he didn't make the White House, his entry into the Presidential race restored him to the top spot on the nation's television, just as the admen intended.

It's no use cats standing for high office if their fellow moggies don't have the vote. Alfred L. Miller managed to put that right in 1977 when he filled in the details on his voter registration form in the American city of Buffalo. Hair: red. Eyes: brown. Place of birth: suburban Tonawanda. Good enough to be accepted as an all-American voter. The only snag was that Alfred L. Miller (Alfie to his friends) was a cat. His owner, Patricia Miller, was making a point. She registered Alfie as a voter "to show how shoddy the mail registration system was".

Alfred L. Miller, registered voter.

The crew of HMS Hecate listed on their 1971 census form a certain "Able Seacat Fred Wunpound, Mouser (second class)".

They were a touch more canny in Scotland, where an attempt to put a cat on the electoral register was foiled by a sharp-eyed official. The crew of HMS *Hecate* listed on their 1971 census form a certain "Able Seacat Fred Wunpound, Mouser (second class)". Back came a letter signed by Mr A. Rennie, Registrar General for Scotland, regretting that Fred could not be included in the Scottish population.

There is, however, evidence in Britain of a desire to find a way round such tiresome rules. In 1975, the Letters page of *The Times* indicated that animal-lovers were striking back in both the hallowed halls of Oxbridge, and from the legal sanctum of the Inner Temple. Kevin J. Marsh wrote from the offices of the Oxford University magazine *Isis* to reveal that "Worcester, like most colleges, does not admit dogs. The Dean's dog, Flint, has thus been officially declared a cat by the Governing Body."

Sir Kenneth Roberts-Wray,QC, wrote of "a legal draftsman in

> *"I have therefore deemed his cat to be a firearm."*

the West Indies who was instructed to prepare a bill for the registration of cats. He simply inserted three words in the Registration of Dogs Ordinance: "Dog includes cat."

And Dr J. Campbell disclosed how they bent the rules in Cambridge. "Sir, I am a Dean of King's College and I have no cat. However, the Praelector keeps a cat within the college. My predecessors have had no explicit power to license cats, but they were entitled to issue permission for the keeping of firearms. I have therefore deemed his cat to be a firearm. I trust, sir, that this information will be helpful."

In America they deemed a cat worthy of a credit rating. Owner Janet Ringgenburg, of Hemet in California, was particularly delighted when a letter from MasterCard/Visa dropped through her letterbox in 1988 offering a five thousand dollar credit limit. You see, Janet had an epileptic condition which forced her to live on state aid - and that, in turn, made it virtually impossible for her to get credit, let alone own a credit card. She thought someone had had a change of heart - until she looked more closely and saw that the letter was addressed to *Fustuce* Ringgenburg - the formal name for Fred, her black and white tomcat. "How," she thought,

> *"How," she thought, "can they deny me a credit card, and give my cat one?"*

"can they deny *me* a credit card, and give my cat one?" It turned out that, a year earlier, Janet's eighteen-year-old daughter Barbara had filled out a detailed questionnaire about the family's buying and eating habits to get coupons for their food. Fred got a prominent mention - and some computer system blindly plucked the cat's name out at random for inclusion in a mailing list that was subsequently picked up by the credit card company. Janet was half-inclined to send away for the credit card - and let Fred do all her shopping for her.

Another case of mistaken identity nearly cost the life of Ginger, an overweight factory tomcat. Reports that a lion or a cougar had been seen prowling through a suburb of the Australian city of

Sydney in 1982 brought the police out in force. A helicopter was called in to help a street-by-street search by twenty men armed with tranquilliser guns. A television news crew followed them, ready to film the action. When finally cornered, the "cougar" turned out to be Ginger, wondering what all the fuss was about!

Some cats have a lot to learn - but few are prepared to go to school to do it. Inky was on the register at a county primary school for six years. When his young mistress started attending classes at Ashby Hill Top Primary in Leicestershire, he decided to go along too - and enjoyed the routine so much that he kept it up after she left. So whenever the bell rang to signal the start of the day's lessons, Inky came running to occupy his favourite spot on top of a cupboard. It was generally assumed that he was after the job of milk monitor. That position eluded him - but he was the only pupil who wasn't shouted at if he happened to doze off. Clearly a cat with a touch of class.

It was generally assumed that he was after the job of milk monitor.

Some animals are happy just to be cats. That can be a shade embarrassing if you happen to be a pig. Baby porker Ben was faced with this identity crisis when he was sat upon rather heavily by one of his uncles. He would have died if Maria Hennessey hadn't saved his bacon. She took him home to her animal sanctuary at Trinant near the South Wales town of Abertillery, and put him in with her four cats. Ben's behavioural pattern underwent a radical change. He became all kittenish - using the cats' litter tray, sharing their food, and even curling up with them in front of the fire. Maria was convinced he thought the cats were his brothers and sisters. She didn't say what it was like to have a pig curled up in her lap!

MᶜLACHLAN

FOR THE LOVE OF A CAT

Italian railways apologised for a twenty-five minute delay in the departure of an express train from Rome's mainline station. But for once the passengers couldn't blame the management or the equipment. An alert conductor, slamming the doors ready for departure, had noticed a cat having kittens between the tracks. The unfortunate moggie hadn't made it home in time. The stationmaster proudly recorded five early arrivals at platform three.

An alert conductor, slamming the doors ready for departure, had noticed a cat having kittens between the tracks.

Cats the world over have the ability to bring life to a halt, touching human emotions in ways that probably say more about the humans than their pets. There is nothing particularly new about that – two thousand years ago Egyptian ladies went through an elaborate ritual of mourning when a much-loved cat died. And it is by no means a one-way relationship.

In 1874, W.H.G. Kingston's *Stories of Animal Sagacity* recorded the tale of a cat that died of grief refusing to leave its owner's grave.

A hundred years later, Michael Stourton bagged two columns of *The Times* to relate in whimsical fashion the tale of a cat that was buried with full military honours. It all began one afternoon when the telephone rang in the orderly room at Wellington Barracks. On the line was a Mrs Strathgarne, who introduced herself as a neighbour, with a flat in Buckingham Gate just opposite the garden of the officers' mess. She explained that every day her beloved cat Fitzroy was in the habit of crossing the road and squeezing through the iron railings to enjoy the space and peace of the officers' garden. And she was able to keep a maternal eye on him from her window. Sadly, Fitzroy had just died, and she had a request which she hoped could be put before the Commanding Officer: "I realise it is expecting a great deal of him, but I wonder if he might agree to Fitzroy being buried in your garden. It would mean so much to me to be able to look on to his little grave; and with your permission I would like to plant a cherry tree to mark the spot". As it happened, the Commanding Officer had already left on a weekend break. His colleagues were somewhat taken with the thought of acceding to the old lady's request, with the proviso that it would have to be at a time on Sunday afternoon "so we don't have too many people wondering what it is all about". Jack Coleford, the duty officer, was given his orders:

"At 14.30 hours on Sunday, accompanied by an orderly, Guardsman Partington, you will meet Mrs Strathgarne at the barrack gate. She will be accompanied by her maid carrying the dead cat in a basket; and by a man from the nursery gardens with the cherry tree. You will direct Mrs Strathgarne and her party to the burial site where Guardsman Jenkins, the officers' mess duty waiter, will be waiting in clean fatigue dress, equipped with a spade. There will be two holes already dug – one for the cat, one for the tree. When the burial has taken place, you will escort Mrs

"Mr Coleford snapped up to the salute and 'eld it there a good minute. Split me up the seams – honest it did."

Strathgarne to the barrack gate – and, if necessary, see her over the road, as she is likely to be in an upset state."

Guardsman Partington later described the ceremony to a senior officer in these terms: "All went according to plan, Sir. Lady arrived spot on time. Tiny little thing she was; all in black. Felt real sorry for her standing there – but Mr Coleford, he was bloody marvellous. Atholl grey coat, forage cap, sword: the lot. Towered over her, 'e did, and when Jenkins lowered the basket into the 'ole, Mr Coleford snapped up to the salute and 'eld it there a good minute. Split me up the seams – honest it did." And, it seems, the cherry tree grows on, "testifying silently and prettily to a military exploit that is unlikely to appear in the regimental history".

Not all organisations adopt such a sympathetic approach. One Saturday in March 1984, rugby full-back John Hickey arrived late for a first XV match between Clifton and Warminster. The vigorous and concisely expressed wrath of his captain was only silenced when Hickey explained that he had suffered a sudden family bereavement. The contrite captain had a word with the referee, and despite a bitterly cold wind the two teams stood in silence for two minutes. After the match someone asked Hickey if the deceased was a very close member of his family. "Certainly was," he replied. "It was my cat". John Hickey's next game was for the third XV.

Eddie and Elaine Yardley from Gatley in Manchester resorted to calling in twenty mediums to help in

the hunt for their much loved ginger tomcat, Steed, who disappeared through the catflap one dark evening never to return. After fruitlessly placing an advertisement in their local paper offering a £250 reward, and distributing a thousand leaflets, they turned in desperation to the psychics. "A few couldn't help," said Elaine. "Some clung to photos of Steed and went into a sort of deep meditation. The rest said Steed is alive, but couldn't say where, and couldn't bring him home. And," she added, "they cost me £200. I had an open mind about their abilities. Now you can't print what I think."

When Norma Dellimore's cat Aaron went missing in Hounslow in Middlesex, she went out hunting for him around her neighbours' houses in the small hours of the morning. Someone spotted her prowling about, and rang the police, who promptly arrested her – just as she had been on the point of catching Aaron.

The increasingly exasperated policemen accepted that she was a cat lover, not a cat burglar.

But Norma wasn't giving up. Three times she went out on Aaron's trail – and on all three occasions she ended up under arrest. The increasingly exasperated policemen accepted that she was a cat lover, not a cat burglar.

John Kitchener, happy owner of both cat and car.

Engineer John Kitchener loved his cat Lucky so much that when the moggy disappeared from his holiday home on Canvey Island in Essex, he offered his luxurious Mercedes car as a reward for anyone who could find him. Fortunately, he didn't have to pay up. Five weeks to the day after the cat vanished, John glimpsed Lucky in his headlights as he came home one evening. The half-starved cat was only too happy to return to the fold.

In 1955, Mrs Rubi Duckworth was greatly

She drove two thousand miles across Europe to be reunited with her cat – only to find it was the wrong cat!

distressed when her marmalade cat, Mr Widdlecombe, sent from Malta to England by air to await her arrival, escaped at London Airport. A massive search was ordered – and a cat answering Mr Widdlecombe's description was found. Mrs Duckworth was so relieved that she drove two thousand miles across Europe to be reunited with her cat – only to find it was the wrong cat! Mr Widdlecombe became one of the few cats to attract the official attention of the British Parliament, actually provoking a question in the House of Commons about his failure to serve the six months in quarantine which all imported animals have to endure in order to keep rabies out of the country.

Prison boss Ernest Price was only too aware of the quarantine rules – they helped to bump up his bill for rescuing a crippled Greek kitten to £1500 – big enough for the *Daily Mirror* to rate the story an "exclusive". On holiday in the resort of Halkidiki, Ernest and his wife Eveline fell instantly in love with the cat they called Zorba. "We saw him scratching for food and water around our hotel. One leg was broken after being kicked by a Greek youth – it is now shorter than the others, and he will always walk with a limp. We were both in tears as we went back home, but we were determined to do what we could to bring Zorba over here." The couple were worried that the cat might starve to death when the hotel closed for the winter – so Ernest, third in command at the Wakefield top security jail in Yorkshire, launched a mission to save him. He left Zorba with a Greek shop girl who promised to look after him, and returned home to work out the best way to get him

It may have been the wrong cat, but it seemed happy enough posing in Mrs Duckworth's arms.

to Britain. Then, after phoning every day to make sure the kitten was alright, Ernest and Eveline returned to Halkidiki for a second package holiday, which ended with them putting Zorba on a plane back to Britain. Along with the required six months in quarantine, it all cost the Prices far more than they expected. But, they said, it was worth every penny, and they promised to make sure Zorba lived in luxury for the rest of his life. The young cat finally arrived at the Price home to discover he would be sharing it with seven chihuahua dogs – a mere trifle of a problem for a cat which had been weaned on scavenging for scraps in the back streets of a Greek town.

Some people love their cats so much they take them on holiday with them – and even officialdom can dip into its corporate pocket to make sure the animals get there. The *Today* newspaper reported how ITN reporter Sarah Cullen and her husband Kieran Devaney paid six pounds for their adopted stray, Teacup, to fly with them from London to their Irish holiday home. But, after landing in Dublin, Aer Lingus refused to carry the cat on to Rosses Point in County Sligo because the hold of the turbo-prop used for the second leg of the journey wasn't pressurised. Instead they forked up £280 to pay for taxis to carry the ginger tom a hundred and twenty miles to his holiday destination, and back again.

An Aer Lingus official said, "Teacup was just like any other passenger."

An Aer Lingus official said, "Teacup was just like any other passenger, and was our responsibility until he reached his destination."

The city of Paris, which already had a law allowing stray cats to be eliminated if they proved to be a nuisance, brought cat lovers out in force when it proposed a "decatification" programme for the French capital in November 1984. Demonstrators took to the streets demanding "equal rights" for cats, and declaring that no-one had the right to organise their deaths because they were "part of the national ecology". The Association for the Protection of Cats

74

Militant cat-lovers on the streets of Paris.

condemned efforts by private firms to round up and kill strays, claiming that they resulted in an illicit trade in fur and whiskers. The protestors suggested that a better way to control the animal population was to insist on having all cats tattooed, with all those allowed out of doors having to be registered at local council offices. Finally they demanded the creation of a new government department devoted to the protection of animals.

Photo opportunity for actress Malisa Longo as she helps attach flea collars in Rome.

Perhaps more typically French was a protest by animal lovers on the Riviera, demanding the release of a seventy-one-year-old madam of a local brothel. But their case would hardly have found favour in a court of law. They argued that Paula Laforge had forty-eight cats in her Nice hotel, and while she was in jail they would starve because there was no-one to feed them!

In Rome, the cat problem wasn't so much a matter of life and death – more a matter of fleas! Their Association for the Protection of Animals started a campaign in 1974 to put an anti-flea collar on every cat in the city.

Britain's RSPCA can hardly have anticipated the passions that would be aroused by its decision to order fifty cats with ringworm to be put down. It ended up sacking an entire branch of the organisation when they refused to obey orders from senior RSPCA inspectors worried that the disease could easily be passed to humans. Members from Colchester sought a second opinion from a local vet, and spent hundreds of pounds having the cats treated. One woman took in twenty-seven of the animals, and even sold her car to pay for heating and medical bills while they were recovering in her garden sheds. The RSPCA's annoyance at such blatant defiance of its experts was tempered by its pleasure that the cats had been cured.

Let's face it, some people are daft about cats – and do some daft things to prove it.

Let's face it, some people are daft about cats – and do some daft things to prove it. Florist Jean Entwhistle was so astounded and delighted when her cat Tinker reached the ripe old age of twenty-one, that she decided to throw a party to celebrate. In 1983 she was reported to have spent two hundred pounds in the local pub at Ramsbottom in Lancashire

Tinker looks a little concerned at apparently being served up as a Lancashire speciality at his own party.

on a champagne party to toast the health of a
cat that, in human terms, was 147 years old.

Londoner Moira Mack was accompanied
by her appropriately named blue cat Tosca
when she spent several days queueing outside
Covent Garden Opera House in 1965 to buy
tickets to hear Maria Callas in the opera of the
same name later in the year. Whether the

feline Tosca required a seat of her own – or even attended the
performance at all – is not revealed. But her presence in the queue
gave her a brief taste of the publicity enjoyed by her namesake.

In 1956 Trenton Raffles, a Blue Persian owned by "a Mrs Norris
of Barnes", took first prize at the Surrey and Sussex Cat Association's

Tosca's vigil.

Plenty of fur still
available on an
indignant Raffles.

Open Show. But it was Mrs Norris
who really stole the show, turning up
in a hat and scarf made from cat fur!
Before you think the worst, let me
tell you that the fur actually came
from the award-winning cat itself.
Mrs Norris was in the habit of saving
the "combings" each time Raffles was
groomed, and having them spun into
soft wool, from which she knitted
her "attractive accessories" (as the
report put it!).

Some owners are often said to
grow to look like their pets. South
African fashion model Chanel Baxter
did it the other way around. She
sent six months searching for a cat
with eyes that matched her own – no
easy task, as Chanel was born with
one eye brown and the other blue.

Made for each
other – Chanel and
Roche.

Eventually a white Persian called Roche turned up to keep both the model and her publicist happy.

Love of cats tends to stick around when love of humans fades. The more spectacular divorce cases in the United States show just how powerful a pull pets can be. When Hollywood make-up artist Ron Britton sued the actress Kim Basinger for divorce, he demanded half of her thirty million pound fortune. She was already paying him 10,000 dollars a month plus regular three thousand dollar mortgage payments on their million-dollar home, which she was happy to let him keep. As well as refusing to pay him any more alimony, the film star had another sticking point – she was determined to retain custody of the ten cats and dogs which the couple had shared. And Hugh Hefner, the boss of *Playboy* magazine, was once reported to be holding a cat hostage at his Californian mansion. He said he wouldn't return Pug to his ex-lover Carrie Leigh until she dropped a twenty million dollar legal action against him.

Soviet-British relations reached a new, if little reported, high in April 1989 – but only just! Under the headline "Purrestroika", *The Times* reported how a London rendezvous between an English and a Russian cat club nearly came to grief because the British Embassy in Moscow withheld visas for the trip. According to one of the Russians, "they didn't believe we were going to do what we said we were going to do." Luckily a cat-loving Foreign Office official intervened to save the day – but not in time to save the leader of the Russian delegation, Mrs Olga Frovlova. She ended up in hospital after tripping over a cat and breaking her leg. The meeting had been set up set up for the Soviets to find out how the British deal with the welfare of cats. This, as *The Times* gently pointed out, "is not a priority in Moscow where stray cats are regarded as hats on legs".

LUCKY BREAKS

I t was the newscaster Reginald Bosanquet who discovered the story first. In an idle moment, he had been browsing through a Ministry of Defence report on how British soldiers had stepped into the breach during a Firemen's strike. The troops had been called upon to man the army's "Green Goddesses" - fire-engines from the Second World War hauled out of mothballs to make sure the country was not left without cover during the long industrial dispute. When it was all over the soldiers had quite a few tales to tell, and the men from the Ministry felt their report would not be complete unless it was laced with a few of their more interesting experiences. Reggie had been drawn to one in particular - and was set on using it round off the evening news. He related it to the late-afternoon programme planning meeting.

A little old lady needed help to rescue her cat from a tree. Neighbours had tried and failed. It was clearly a job for the "Green Goddess". Arriving with speed and panache, the soldiers sprang into action, and within minutes the little old lady had been reunited with her beloved cat. Her garden was filled with people offering congratulations. So grateful was the little old lady that she insisted on inviting the entire crew of the Green Goddess into her parlour for tea and home-made cakes, which they hugely enjoyed. Half an hour later, with the little old lady's gratitude still ringing in their ears, the soldiers emerged from the house, jumped into the Green Goddess, reversed down the drive, and promptly ran over the cat!

That was the story, and the then editor, Nigel Ryan, allowed Reggie to include it in the bulletin on one condition - if even a hint of a smile crossed his face while he was reading it, he would be sacked! Spoken at least half in jest, it was a wise precaution. Even without the smile, the ITV switchboards were jammed for the best part of an hour

If even a hint of a smile crossed his face while he was reading it, he would be sacked!

Cat up a tree –
Jeremy on his
lofty perch.

afterwards, as British viewers split evenly into two opposing camps. Half of the callers thought it was just about the funniest thing they had ever heard; the other half protested angrily at what they saw as a shameful attempt to extract humour from the death of a cat. Clearly, the editor had been wise to remove the traditional end-of-bulletin smile on the face of the newscaster. Its absence enabled him to point out in defence that Reggie had simply reported, without comment, an extract from a Ministry of Defence document. It provided the required journalistic alibi for arguably the most controversial of cat stories ever broadcast - although you can still find those prepared to swear they detected just a flicker of a smirk before the studio lights dimmed and Reggie said "Goodnight".

Fortunately for cats, not all lucky breaks have a sting in the tail. In March 1974, a six-month-old moggy called Jeremy was a touch over-enthusiastic in his pursuit of a bird, and ended up stuck at the top of a sixty-five-foot tree in Seven Sisters Road in North London. The RSPCA decided the only way to rescue him was to lasso the tree and shake him out. Unfortunately, as he fell Jeremy missed the sheet carefully stretched out to catch him, and sustained injuries which took several months to mend. In fact, it would appear that the only part of him which did not recover was his memory - within days of the vet giving him a clean bill of health, he belted up to the top of the tree again. This time the RSPCA took

Within days of the vet giving him a clean bill of health, he belted up to the top of the tree again.

a more relaxed, long-term view and decided to starve him down.

It was almost a re-run of an incident twenty-five years earlier when, for five days, a cat clung to a branch sixty feet above St Paul's Road, Islington. Instead of a lasso, a fireman went up to saw through the branch, while his colleagues below optimistically held out a sheet. As the branch fell, the cat leapt - missed the sheet, landed (without any apparent injury) and made off. This rare insight into a cat's enforced flying technique was captured by an alert photographer.

A miscalculation by both cat and firemen.

Fortunately, no-one has tested the maximum height from which a cat can fall - and survive. But Benji the tabby must come close to the record. Pouncing on a pigeon outside his owners' tenth-floor flat in East London, he missed and tumbled over the edge. An amazed resident saw him passing her window, and looked out to find that a clump of rose bushes had broken Benji's fall. She was even more amazed when the caretaker returned the cat to his owners, apparently none the worse for wear.

Pouncing on a pigeon outside his owners' tenth-floor flat in East London, he missed and tumbled over the edge.

Henry the cat had rather less far to fall when he slid off a roof in Cheltenham. But he got stuck upside down in a tiny gap between two buildings. Firemen had to chip away cement and brickwork to get him out - leaving his owners with an expensive repair bill.

He was lucky. A Manchester cat called Marcus spent three and a half weeks bricked up in a wall in 1984. He slipped through a hole while council workmen were repairing an air vent and became trapped in the cavity between the inner and outer walls. Eventually his cries were heard by his owner, fifteen-year-old Sarah Bower, who had spent days searching for him. The RSPCA said Marcus

Marcus explains
his ordeal to Sarah
Bower, his
relieved owner.

probably lived off spiders, woodlice, and
(if he was lucky) an occasional passing
mouse. He must also have had some
access to rain water. But the key to his
survival was probably the enormous
amount of surplus body fat he carried
with him. At the time of his
disappearance, Marcus weighed twenty-
eight pounds! When found he was not
only wiser, but a mere shadow of his
former self.

Six years passed before his record was broken by Cleo from
North Tyneside, who disappeared when her owners, John and
Kathy McKay, moved into a new housing estate. A full month later,
the owners of a bungalow being built in the next close were looking
over their new home when they heard strange sounds coming from
beneath their feet. The floorboards were lifted - to reveal one
bedraggled, skinny cat with quite remarkable powers of survival.

Lucky the kitten was trapped for a mere fourteen hours, but
caused infinitely more chaos for the Sayle family from Miles
Platting near Manchester. Chasing a ball in the family's kitchen, he
fell down a wide ceramic tube encasing the main water-
supply pipe. The tube was so slippery he couldn't climb
back up. To reach him, the fire brigade had to rip up patio
flagstones outside the kitchen window, hack through several
feet of concrete, and smash the pipe. In the process they
fractured the main soilpipe to the house, which meant that
until it was repaired, Marion and Thomas Sayle and his
eighty-three-year-old mother Pat couldn't use the lavatory,
the bath or any of the sinks. Such an experience made
them wonder whether it really was wise to have as many as
six cats and seven kittens. So, after all the chaos he caused,
Lucky and most of his friends found themselves looking

*To reach him, the
fire brigade had to
rip up patio
flagstones outside
the kitchen
window, hack
through several
feet of concrete,
and smash the
pipe.*

for new homes.

Barney disappeared down new sewage pipes being laid to houses at North Tawton in Devon. His owner, Gill Tregunna, gave him up for lost. Thirteen days later he turned up inside one of the houses to which the pipes were being laid. Barney had somehow crawled up the pipe, negotiated the U-bend and emerged from the lavatory bowl - presumably before it was operational! So the tabloid writers were employing just a touch of artistic licence with the headline "Soggy Mog Flushed Out".

A carpet company in the Ulster town of Donaghadee was accustomed to sending its products all over the world - but it wasn't in the habit of carrying passengers. That changed when one large consignment, carefully wrapped in plastic, arrived at one of the firm's distribution points at Blackburn in Lancashire. A loader was about to drive a steel rod down the tube at the centre of one roll of carpet when foreman Ron Tee heard a faint miaowing, and ordered work to be stopped. Inside was a tiny kitten who had survived the wrapping process and the buffeting of the overnight ferry across the Irish Sea. The stowaway was promptly named Paddy, and offered a new home with the firm's security officer.

Paddy emerges from his roll of carpet.

Curiosity nearly killed JR, a kitten belonging to Rochdale schoolboy Paul Harrison. Paul had taken his elderly Hoover vacuum cleaner to bits for a DIY dusting and service. When he nipped out of the room for a second,

Foreman Ron Tee heard a faint miaowing, and ordered work to be stopped.

JR in the Hoover, and (below) Bosley after the spin.

He sneaked in through the open door of the front loader for a nap on a bundle of towels.

JR nipped in - into the Hoover, that is - and stayed mum while it was being reassembled. In fact, he didn't start complaining until the machine was switched on, and the poor kitten was sucked into some part of its inner workings where even he would have been reluctant to venture. Getting out proved as difficult as getting in. Five firemen failed to free him. So the Hoover was sacrificed - cracked open like an egg to reunite JR and Paul.

Bosley - from Brigg near Humberside - must have thought he was all washed up after a spin in a washing machine. He sneaked in through the open door of the front loader for a nap on a bundle of towels. Owner Gillian Burnett came back, slammed the door shut, switched on the machine - and then went shopping. It was only when her husband John spotted something black and white thumping around in the machine that he was released. The unfortunate Bosley had been subjected to a warm pre-wash, a spin, a cold rinse, and the best (or worst) part of a hot wash. The vet gave the unconscious cat an injection, and when he revived eight hours later he was as perky as ever. The theme is a recurring one in newspaper stories about cats. Mercifully we only hear about the washing-machined cats that survive - like Twinkle the tortoiseshell, Pat Scott's cat from Slough in Berkshire. Pat was poised to give him the kiss of life, but Twinkle came out covered in lather and none the worse for wear. And, for some reason not

fully explained, Maureen Perrin, from Rainham in Kent, summoned the local fire brigade to *cut open* her washing machine, where her kitten was being boil-washed. Cats really do have to learn to clean themselves - no matter how much longer it takes!

What is truly astounding is the number of times that firemen are called into action to rescue cats. They clearly don't spend nearly as much time fighting fires as we all thought! In April 1987, Swansea fire brigade just couldn't get away from cats even when they were summoned to tackle a blaze. Five minutes out of the fire station with siren whining, light flashing and tyres squealing, they routinely checked a locker to find that three kittens had just been born on top of one of their hoses. How they handled this delicate emergency, or how it affected their capacity to fight the fire, is not reported.

They routinely checked a locker to find that three kittens had just been born on top of one of their hoses.

The prize for the most ridiculous genuine reason for summoning the fire brigade probably goes to Philip Edmonds of Haywards Heath in Sussex. He called to say that his moggy, Looby-Lou, was hanging from the letter box. She had apparently jumped up to try to catch something and had got her paw stuck.

Builder Alan Exley came home from work in the Yorkshire town of Penistone to find that a cat and the fire brigade had, between them, destroyed his car. Tim the kitten had crept under the eight-year-old Renault and jammed himself in a tiny space. Summoned by Alan's wife Joanne, the firemen said there was no alternative - they would have to cut Tim free. Out came the power saw, cutting through a floor panel and the chassis! And then the firemen beat a hasty retreat, leaving Joanne to do the explaining. "I thought she was joking at first," said Alan. "Then I blew my top. But when I calmed down I couldn't stop laughing."

Janet and Adrian Barnfather had some trouble seeing the funny side when their cat Bing was trapped under their neighbour's car bonnet. Four miles down the road, in Fairburn near Wakefield, a passer-by spotted Bing's head poking out, and a vet and a team of mechanics struggled for two hours to free him. They eventually had to dismantle the entire front of the car - leaving Bing to recover from a gash on his paw, and the Barnfathers to recover from the hundred pound bill for freeing him.

Of course, cats do occasionally travel quite legitimately by car. Dark Stranger, a black Persian owned by Mrs MacDonald from Holywood in County Down, was on his way to a show in the North of England when their car was involved in a sixty-mile-an-hour accident on the M1 motorway. Mrs MacDonald escaped with scratches, but had to go to hospital for a check-up. Dark Stranger's box was hurled forward and smashed by the impact. Unhurt,

Unhurt, but terrified, the cat dashed across six lanes of high-speed traffic and disappeared.

Dark Stranger, a particularly lucky black cat.

but terrified, the cat dashed across six lanes of high-speed traffic and disappeared. Released from hospital, Mrs MacDonald returned to the spot, but failed to find him and returned to Northern

Ireland. Two weeks later she heard that her cat had been killed on the motorway, but, refusing to believe it, returned to the spot and, by chance, saw Dark Stranger in the distance. The Luton RSPCA lent her a baited trap, and she managed to catch him. Carrying on to London, she gave her cat a quick brush-up and decided to enter him for the 1966 Southern Counties Cat Club show, for which he had been originally entered. Dark Stranger took the top prize - not in itself enough to get him into the news. It was his long, unusual journey to victory which did that!

From Finland, in 1963, came the story of a cat who survived all her owner's attempts to put her down. In the original translation, it reads almost like a fairytale. "Killi is a three-year-old she-cat, friend and companion of a little girl living on the sixth floor of a big tenement house in Helsinki. But as the little girl grew into a young girl, and found other friends and companions, keeping Killi in a small city flat became too much of a bother; and so the young girl's father took the cat to a place where animals are put to a painless death. He paid the modest sum which is asked for this kind of service, and was told to come back the next day to collect the corpse. When he returned he found Killi in a corner, bloody, with her nose broken and a claw loose, but very much alive. He was told to pay an additional fee and return again the following day when the matter would be settled once and for all. But they did not know the fighting spirit that was in Killi. A policeman with helmet and gloves was finally called, and still Killi went victorious out of the fight. After returning four times in vain to the place where Killi was supposed to meet a quick and painless death, her owner could stand it no longer. 'Okay, you win,' he said to the cat, and back home they went, Killi riding in triumph in the taxi. Now she strolls the small rooms of the flat again in the proud knowledge that she has fully earned the privilege of being alive."

Killi lives on!

Minnie spent forty-eight hours inside the forty-five-foot beast.

You would be a touch sceptical if you saw a story about a cat ending up inside a dinosaur. But one moggy did get trapped inside a model dinosaur at Dan Yr Ogof caves near Swansea. Minnie spent forty-eight hours inside the forty-five-foot beast, which she entered by climbing scaffolding put up for repairs. She was rescued by Steven Griffiths, an instructor on a nearby ski slope and an experienced caver, who wriggled inside with a rope.

"Hiss of Life for Cat" said the headline, after a cat locked inside a

Miaow!

To stop the cat suffocating, the jeweller used the pump to blow puffs of air through the tiny keyhole.

jeweller's safe in Toulon in France was saved by a bicycle pump. To stop the cat suffocating, the jeweller used the pump to blow puffs of air through the tiny keyhole. And he had to keep puffing for two days, while a pre-set electronic timing device protected the million pounds worth of jewels keeping the cat company. "My cat," said the jeweller, "is more precious to me than all the gems."

88

MONSTER MOGGIES

A nineteenth-century lithograph, entitled simply *Large Cat*, records what it describes as "this noble specimen, domesticated at 175, Oxford Street...very docile, though his unusually large size conveys to the beholder, at first sight, a contrary impression". Despite his weight, meticulously measured at twenty-five and three-quarter pounds, the seven-year-old cat was said to be "extremely active, and rarely inconvenienced by his great bulk".

Public fascination with oversize domestic cats has grown with time, the media being keen to balance the curiosity value of such freaks with assurances that the weighty specimens were well looked after. There appears to be some sensitivity to mentioning that such cats invariably have hormonal or genetic problems, or are grossly overfed. But any delicacy or doubts about the wisdom of thrusting these monster moggies into the public gaze has long since vanished. It is now open season on the cats whose photographs appear to provoke instant delight or disgust in equal measure.

Fox Photos, a freelance agency, were among the first to enter the fray. In 1938

Any delicacy or doubts about the wisdom of thrusting these monster moggies into the public gaze has long since vanished.

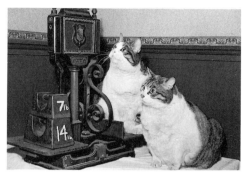

they pictured a Sheffield caretaker, Mr E. Kay, with his *twenty-one* pound cat, Bill – more than double the normal weight. Described as "a giant among cats", he measured twenty-seven inches round the chest, and thirty-seven inches from front paws to back paws (which were themselves three inches across). And over the next half century bids to beat that flowed in with impressive regularity, as "big cat" owners came out of the closet. Tearoom owner Mary Kennedy, from the Scottish town of Ayr, managed to double the figure – but took *two* cats to do

Eight-year-old twins Dusty and Rusty tipped the scales at twenty-one pounds each.

it. Eight-year-old twins Dusty and Rusty tipped the scales at twenty-one pounds *each*. And they were just the ones we were told about! Their mother, also a heavyweight puss, had almost two hundred kittens in her lifetime.

London firemen who turned out to fight a restaurant fire in High Holborn in 1936 found themselves rescuing Ginger, described in a newspaper report the next day as "the heaviest cat in London". He was promptly challenged for the title by Billy of Lancaster Gate, whose mere twenty-*three* pounds weren't quite good enough. Ginger beat him by a whisker – in his case about half a pound! Nevertheless it was close enough to teach newspapers not to make extravagant claims, and by the time another Ginger hove into view – taking a Reserve Award in the Household section of the 1967 Herts and Middlesex Cat Show – his twenty-*six* pounds did no more than earn him the title of "heaviest cat in the show".

Brought up with Fritz, a mild-mannered mongrel, he sees off the dog's enemies with just a flick of his fearsome tail.

Another twenty-eight pounder, Joseph, inherited £365 in his mistress's will.

Twenty-*eight* pounds – along with twenty-eight inches around the middle and a tough personality to boot – earned Tibby, from Northfleet in Kent, a job guarding a dog. Brought up with Fritz, a mild-mannered mongrel, he sees off the dog's enemies with just a flick of his fearsome tail. A tiny, bedraggled kitten when found by Hilda Dodd, tubby twelve-year-old Tibby was brought up on liver and hearts. He needed four good meals a day to keep him going – nearly twice as many as Fritz.

Joseph strikes a regal pose.

Another twenty-eight pounder, Joseph, inherited £365 in his mistress's will. Just by looking at him, you know he's going to blow it all on food!

Then there was Tiddles, a *thirty*-pound cat who used to stretch across two plastic chairs at London's Paddington Station until he died at the ripe old age of twenty-four. Attendant June Watson took pity on him when, as a tiny kitten, he wandered into the ladies' loo in search of a square meal. She can

Mrs Maynard's
Tiddles displays
his ample girth.

hardly have guessed when she started him off with a piece of cheese from her sandwich that Tiddles would end up three feet long and one foot wide, thanks to regular supplies of steak, chicken, liver, kidneys and rabbit – food which, in later years, was stored in his own special fridge. When voted London's "Fat Cat Champion" in 1983, Tiddles was getting a touch slow on his paws. Not that it mattered – he had never been known to catch a mouse!

Even he might have quaked if it had been possible to bring him face-to-face with his namesake – an eight-year-old tomcat owned by Mary Maynard of Wymondham in Norfolk. But time as well as distance prevented such an encounter. *This* Tiddles was reported to be Britain's biggest cat in 1959. Also extremely good-natured – and who wouldn't be with a life that revolved around eating and sleeping - he weighed in at *thirty-six* pounds. Will no-one bid any more? Do I hear *thirty-seven*?

Paws up, Thomas O'Malley, billed as "the King Kong of the cat world" in 1977. His waist was two inches bigger than that of his mistress, Hilda John, who brought him up from a kitten in her Cardiff home. She couldn't understand how he grew so big, because his mother, brothers and sisters were all of normal size.

Thomas apparently opened doors with his paws – and when he wanted to come in from the garden he rapped the door knocker. Mrs John reckoned he was better than a watchdog, claiming that when he was disturbed at night his purring was louder than any doorbell. "People," she said, "often mistake him for a dog. The gasman once said 'That corgi of yours hasn't moved all the time I've been here.'"

"People," she said, "often mistake him for a dog."

And there lies the problem. Few cats that reach such colossal size are exactly quick on their feet. Given the option – and a human or three to attend to their every need – they take the line of least resistance, find a cosy spot and just stay there.

Three of the biggest! Welsh contender Thomas O'Malley (above left), old champion Ginger from High Holborn (above) and filling the frame (left) Tiddles of Paddington.

An early heavyweight champion of the cat world was Tiger, a mighty moggy from Billericay in Essex. The *Guinness Book of Records* awarded him the title after sending down officials to weigh and measure him. Thirty-three and a half inches around the waist, and fourteen and a half inches around the neck, Tiger tipped the scales at three stone – that's a colossal forty-two pounds. His owner Gill Dacey put it down to his extreme laziness and a gourmet diet. No tinned

No tinned food for this highly pampered pet. He would only touch fresh cod and stewing steak.

food for this highly pampered pet. He would only touch fresh cod and stewing steak. His size was only matched by his timidity – the only time he carted his portly frame off with any speed was when he was running away from a mouse!

But even Tiger could have hidden in the shadow of Himmy, a neutered male tabby owned by Thomas Vyse from Cairns in Queensland. So heavy he had to be carried around in a wheelbarrow, Himmy was just three quarters of an ounce short of forty-six pounds. Three feet two inches long, he measured thirty-three inches round the neck. Not surprisingly, he died of respiratory failure in March 1986.

Ship's Cats

"Conquering Cat" proclaimed *The Times* of 9 March 1960, as its correspondent, reporting from a ship on duty in the Red Sea, offered a no-nonsense description of the proper working relationship between sailor and cat. "Tiger came aboard in Djibouti, French Somaliland. He was not invited, but just walked over the gangway of the cable-ship, of which I was Third Officer at the time, as if it belonged to him. He paid no attention to anyone in the way of greeting, but got straight to work catching rats and eating them. No 'cat-and-mouse' games but serious business. We had the rats – *he* wanted them, and he caught and ate them. That suited us all right, so we allowed him to stay."

Tao-Tai, an essential fixture on the *Sagamore*.

So vital a part of a vessel do ships' cats become that, in 1975, Furness Withy, one of Britain's largest shipping groups, actually included a cat amongst the "fixtures and fittings" on board a 15,500-ton cargo ship, the *Sagamore*, which they were selling to an Italian group for half a million pounds. The Siamese, Princess Truban Tao-Tai, had been taken on board by a former captain sixteen years earlier. Since then she had covered more than one and a half million miles – never setting a paw ashore because of quarantine restrictions. As Furness Withy put it at the time: "She is coming to the twilight of her life, and we didn't want to see her destroyed – so we appealed to the Italians to take her over and look after her." But the Italians didn't want Tao-Tai, and, for a while, it looked as though she might have to be put down. But Furness Withy

"We had the rats – he wanted them, and he caught and ate them. That suited us all right, so we allowed him to stay."

stuck to their guns, inserting a special clause in the sale contract specifiying that the new owners had to "guarantee to keep the cat happy". Finally, the Italians agreed, and the deal went through.

Some cats have little time for the legal niceties. They just make it plain that they are not leaving. In 1953, when the *Discovery* – that famous old ship that carried Scott to the Antarctic – was owned by the Scouts, they found themselves unable to afford the three thousand pounds a year upkeep. The Admiralty expressed an interest in the historic vessel, but they insisted on a proper structural survey. The decks and cabins were cleared – but Beeps, the ship's cat, refused to leave. Having never been ashore since he was a tiny kitten, he had no intention of starting in his old age.

Right
Beeps stands firm in the galley of the *Discovery*.

Nor had the cat which refused to abandon ship even when it hit the rocks. On 17 January 1952, the Liberian freighter *Liberty* went aground near Land's End and was abandoned by her thirty-eight-man crew. But for the next forty-four days the ship's cat refused to leave. Avoiding the traps and resisting the blandishments of the salvage workers, his obstinate courage earned him the nickname

Having never been ashore since he was a tiny kitten, he had no intention of starting in his old age.

"Carlsen" after the gallant skipper of the *Flying Enterprise* who had also refused to leave his post. He was finally captured by the chief salvage officer as a fire which had broken out on the bridge was being extinguished. Determined to the last, Carlsen bit his rescuer sharply on the hand.

A disgruntled Carlsen is re-introduced to his equally uncertain rescuer.

In some countries, even if cats wanted to leave ship, they wouldn't be allowed to. When the cargo ship SS *Coulbeg* arrived at London's Surrey Commercial Docks in January 1951, an emergency call was put out to the People's Dispensary for Sick Animals for a specialist to be sent to examine Paddy, the ship's cat mascot who had been injured during the voyage. The strict quarantine rules prevented Paddy going ashore to see a vet – so Mr Donald Fossey of the PDSA and his staff drove to the docks in their

Paddy receives
attention from the
PDSA vet on board
SS *Coulbeg*.

ambulance, examining and treating the cat aboard ship.

Perhaps cats like their seaborne life so much because they have heard what happens to seafaring cats when they are persuaded onto dry land. All nautical moggies are no doubt indoctrinated with the tale of Susan, the mascot of HMS *Belfast*, who was present for the Second World War assault on the Normandy beaches. She was absolutely terrified when demobbed into life as a landlubber – distraught to find a floor that did *not* have a slight swell to it, and quite terrified of *grass*.

Or perhaps they like life on the ocean wave, not in order to chase mice and rats, but because of the opportunities which all that fresh salt air offers for really deep sleep! Whisky, a tabby who was the mascot of HMS *Duke of York*, distinguished herself by sleeping soundly all the way through the major naval action in which her ship sank the German battlecruiser *Scharnhorst*. Though perhaps she did not quite have the style of the cat based on HMS *Shropshire*, whose tiny personal hammock isolated her from the rigours of too rough a voyage.

Sleeping quarters on the *Shropshire*

Another reason cats inhabit so many ships is undoubtedly because of the superstitious nature of sailors through the ages. That superstition is regularly reinforced by new tales of things going wrong when cats "miss the boat". Take Fred Wunpound, for example – yes – he of Scottish census fame (*see page 66*). This Able Seacat never missed a single voyage for all of his eight years and quarter of a million miles on board HMS *Hecate*. Somehow he always seemed to know when the ship was about to sail, and would appear from nowhere to scurry up the gangplank in the nick of time. Until one voyage from Plymouth to the Hebrides when he just didn't make his departure slot. *Cat World* catalogued the ensuing disasters. "During that trip the ship's computer system broke down; one of the engines developed a fault; the ship's washing machine packed up; the potato peeler in the galley broke down; and another of the ship's engines blew up." When HMS Hecate limped into Stornoway, her captain rushed two of his sailors off to Portsmouth to find Fred and bring him back. From then on – as a precaution – Fred was locked in the library the night before sailing to make sure he didn't get left behind ever again.

The closest the Royal Navy has got to institutionalising

From then on – as a precaution – Fred was locked in the library the night before sailing.

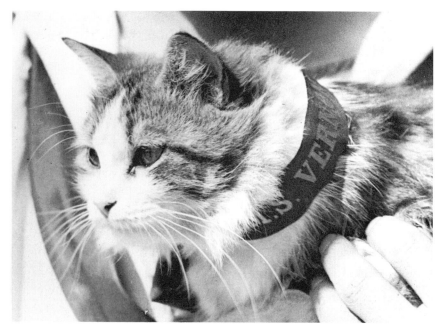

The cat from HMS *Vernon* – possibly the only cat to ever wear a collar.

the role of their cats was an official announcement that "all cats in naval establishments must wear collars at all times". It was backed up by an order signed on behalf of the Lords Commissioners of the Admiralty warning that "all cats found in naval establishments without collars are to be summarily dealt with". The Navy countered with a simple question, guaranteed to send any politician white: "Who will pay for the collars?" The Admiralty remained silent; no grant was forthcoming from the Treasury who, true to form, were playing it tough. The order was quietly dropped.

But when it comes to saying goodbye to a long-serving naval cat, no effort is spared. Charlie was a full member of staff at the HMS *Pembroke* offices at Chatham naval base in Kent. The wages book recorded him as receiving food and lodging. He even had his own security pass. So when he was run over by a car, it seemed only natural to lower the flag to half-mast while a bugler played the Last Post, and the officer of the watch conducted a funeral service complete with full naval honours.

PLUTOCATS AND PRICELESS PUSSIES

When two California cats walk up the aisle to be formally married, you might be forgiven for thinking that Hollywood, on the brink for so long, has finally flipped its lid. In the state where wild excesses have become routine, this is the daddy - or rather, the husband and wife - of them all. Dawn Rogers is presiding over her seventeenth pet wedding. The proud owners happily part with thirty-five dollars to see their cats joined together in outrageous matrimony.

And before that? Perhaps a preparatory visit to a cat bathing salon in Sacramento, where it costs ten dollars to have your cat washed, dried and fluffed. "Nails trimmed? Of course, madam. And would 'sir' prefer the flea-killing shampoo?" The owners, Jack and Willie Martin, come over strong with soothing chat whenever nervous customers face bath-time. And the assistants who blow-dry the customers have been provided with special masks to help avoid flying fur. And to think it all used to be done with a cat's own tongue!

If the thought of all this turns any cats queasy, they can always pop along to the East West Animal Clinic in Oakland, California. On offer here is an alternative to conventional medicine. Owners with deep pockets can now consult veterinary acupuncturists and homeopaths. While one Siamese cat was being examined, and treated

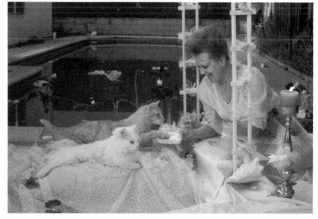

Poolside ceremony in Hollywood.

The assistants who blow-dry the customers have been provided with special masks to help avoid the flying fur.

Above

A champagne lifestyle for Russ but he still prefers milk to 'bubbly'.

Above right

The highly-bred but temeramental Minou Du Coin Vert confronts the cameras.

under anaesthetic, it didn't know it was being eyed by a boa constrictor with a liver complaint! Which could add up to a case for some pretty good health insurance.

Russ the nine-year old Russian Blue was insured for twenty thousand pounds in 1969 - a sum that just about equalled his earnings at that time from commercials, films, television series and guest spots. It added up to a wise investment by animal trainer Clive Desmond, who paid fifteen pounds for Russ as a kitten.

Four years earlier, Yorkshire breeder Shirley Beever spent a mighty two hundred and fifty pounds on quarantine, hotels, phone calls and purchase of Minou Du Coin Vert, a Chartreux or Carthusian cat with magnificent blue fur. The hope was that his kittens would have all of their Dad's show-winning qualities and intelligence.

Similar dedication to breeding produced Magi, the aristocratic Siamese owned by Princess Michael of Kent. The *Daily Telegraph* reported that "he outranks even the Buckingham Palace corgis in the length of his pedigree, which stretches back to one of the original Siamese cats, Tiam O'Shian". Presented to a British

"He outranks even the Buckingham Palace corgis in the length of his pedigree,"

diplomat's wife by the King of Siam, Tiam was mated with Susan, a breeding queen brought in from Bangkok in 1883.

But the real determination to preserve this fine lineage was shown during the Second World War when, it was reported, "owners had to queue for fish or meat bits for their cats. It was also hard to find petrol to visit a stud. Some women used to put their queen in the cycle shed and set off for miles to find one"!

Breeding needs to be protected in other ways too. When Marcus, a seven year old-white Persian described as "the world's top feline", arrived in Glasgow for the Scottish Cat Club Championship Show, he was given VIP treatment - a security guard of his very own. His owner, Elspeth Sellar, wasn't taking any chances with a cat valued at over two thousand pounds.

Marcus and his entourage.

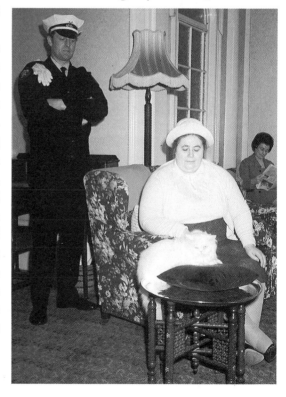

Some cats are born rich - and some have richness thrust upon them. With Tibby, the black and white tomcat on the housing estate at Teddington in Middlesex, it really was touch-and-go. Some housewives noticed him prowling around about the time that Pamplin Vintner, a wealthy chartered accountant, died. Mr Vintner left sixteen thousand pounds to his three cats; but one of them escaped when friends and relatives called at the house. Neighbours claimed that Tibby was that cat. Geoffrey Wright, a local solicitor charged with finding a home for the two remaining cats, promised to contact a friend of Mr Vintner's to check if Tibby was indeed "one of the heirs".

In 1983, a spokesman for the Public Trustees said it was "unusual though not unique" for animal lovers to leave all their money to their pets". Since then the habit has caught on in an increasingly big way. Retired railway clerk, Harry Stivelman, a lonely man who had only his five cats to keep him company, left them his entire estate of £65,000. But that paled into insignificance compared to the impact of a stray cat called Pussy when he walked through an open window of a house belonging to Dorothy Walker, an elderly widow. As her housekeeper told *Today* in 1988, "she just doted on Pussy. He had the most comfortable chair in the lounge and a wonderful life. She fed him all the best cat food, and all she wanted before she died was to ensure that he went to a good home". And who better to guarantee that than the RSPCA. They were staggered to find that Mrs Walker had left them three million pounds in properties and securities - the only condition being that they looked after Pussy for the rest of her days. *Today*, eager to explain the enormity of the sum in terms that cat-loving readers would understand, worked out that the money would keep an average moggy for 2,236 years. It would pay lifetime vet's bills for ten thousand cats, or buy 300,000 cat flaps.

"That," millionaire Ben Rea told a friend at the time, "will look like chickenfeed compared to what I'm going to leave my cats." Two days later he died, giving his *seven* million pound fortune to Blackie, the last of his fifteen cats, and three cat charities.

"That will look like chickenfeed compared to what I'm going to leave my cats."

104

HIGH MILEAGE CATS

Evidence that cats have homing instincts is sketchy to say the least. Many of Britain's million strays are listed as "missing from home", unable or unwilling to return. But there have been so many stories of cats making extraordinary journeys back to their old haunts that scientists at London's Royal Veterinary College decided to launch a proper investigation. The *Daily Express* described how its readers had been "called upon to help by supplying first-hand information about the homing exploits of their cats". The report was written by the renowned specialist in matters of national security, Chapman Pincher – more accustomed to writing about MI5 than CAT. Puzzled *Express* readers seeking an explanation were offered a possible clue in the fourth paragraph: "When thirty-seven Belgian cats reached home within a day of being released twenty miles away, it was seriously planned to train cats *to carry secret messages* as pigeons do." What's more, he went on, "a scientist painlessly anaesthetised a cat and took it on a train journey in a closed basket to a place two hundred miles away. When it woke up, it homed in four days, apparently in a beeline, *as though it had a compass in its head*."

But Mr Pincher did admit that the evidence was conflicting. "Another scientist convinced himself that cats

"It was seriously planned to train cats to carry secret messages as pigeons do."

cannot sense the North. He found that when cats were put in a simple maze, and were allowed out only at the north exit, they were unable to go to that exit directly, even after practising for eighty-five days." To try and solve the mystery, Mr Arthur Marable, a zoologist working with Professor James McCunn, head of the anatomy department, appealed for details of high-mileage journeys involving cats. He could have done worse than comb the pages of the world's newspapers, to whom such stories are meat and drink!

Smoky, a black bob-tailed cat, was reported to have homed three hundred miles from Bexhill in Kent to Newquay in Cornwall in fourteen days. Another homesick moggy, Snoopy, was so upset when his owners, Edna and Leslie Phillips, moved house to Blackpool that he walked the hundred and twenty miles back to his old home at Telford in Shropshire.

In 1988, the French news agency Sipa Press waxed lyrical about "The Incredible Journey of Gribouille the Cat", who took two years to cover a thousand kilometres, crossing international borders, bridges, highways and rivers. When Gribouille was a kitten, his owner, seventy-six-year-old Mme Martinet, gave him to a gendarme whose house was close to her own. A few weeks later this neighbour was transferred from the town of Tannay, in the Central French province of Nièvre, to Reutlingen, near Stuttgart in south-west Germany. He took the kitten with him, and three weeks later wrote to Mme Martinet to let her know that Gribouille had disappeared. Twenty-one months later, a half-starved, skinny cat with sore feet and infected eyes showed up on Mme Martinet's doorstep. She didn't recognise him as the little kitten that had gone missing – but "Gribouille's mother knew her own flesh and blood! She immediately rushed over and began to lick him with much-needed maternal care. Gribouille headed for his own favourite resting spot on the thyme plants at the foot of a plum tree – another sure sign that he was the prodigal feline son." Sipa Press could well have left the story there, but their reporter was moved to new heights of

The amazing reunion of Gribouille and Mme Martinet.

rhetoric – and possibly imagination – by the tender scene. He rounded his narrative off with an emotional flourish: "'Gribouille,' Mme Martinet said softly. He immediately went over to his old mistress, confirming in her mind that it was indeed him. And tears spilled out of the eyes of the young cat: he hadn't heard his name for two years!"

"And tears spilled out of the eyes of the young cat: he hadn't heard his name for two years!"

Not to be outdone, the Soviet newspaper *Komsomolskaya Pravda* found its own version of this perennial tale closer to home. A grey and white cat, Murka, caught and killed her first canary when the bird was out of its cage at the Moscow home of Mr Vladimir Dontsov. A few months later, her appetite clearly whetted, she somehow managed to open the door of the birdcage and devour a second canary. Her punishment was immediate exile to the home of the Dontsov children's grandmother in Voronezh, some four hundred miles away. But Murka stayed at the grandmother's house for only two days before disappearing. A full year later Mr Dontsov was leaving home for work when he recognised the cat near his doorway. Dirty, hungry, pregnant – with an injured ear and minus part of her tail – Murka was home. Reluctant to leave even such an apolitical story without a sideswipe at the bureaucracy of Soviet life, *Komsomolskaya Pravda* marvelled that "without any information desk, she had found her way to the correct neighbourhood"!

The homing instinct is not necessarily the only motive for long cat treks. Back in Paris, Agence France Presse reported that the Servoz family, who lost their pet cat Gringo the previous December, learnt in July that he was living happily at their summer home on the French Riviera. Apparently unable to stand the cold winter, he covered the four hundred and eighty miles in a week, and was being cared for by neighbours who remembered him from previous summer holidays.

Dirty, hungry, pregnant – with an injured ear and minus part of her tail – Murka was home.

A few cats are not above taking some of the leg-work out of their travelling arrangements. In 1958, Dick, a fluffy white tomcat, hitch-hiked a two-hundred-and-fifty-mile ride on a lorry from Bideford in Devon. He apparently sat the whole way on the spare wheel under the chassis, risking death with every bump as the open road flashed past beneath. He was spotted on arrival at Hillingdon in Middlesex – wet, muddy, but unhurt – and was taken to a nearby RSPCA centre to await the arrival of his anxious owner.

Kitty, another young hitch-hiker who travelled seven miles on the back axle of her owner's van.

A ten-week-old kitten who'd had enough of the London "cat race" chose an equally novel way to leave town – clinging to the chassis of a train. Amid jokes about "fur-dodging" , and with "intercity kitty" providing the required headline alliteration, Fleet Street described how he had travelled beneath the ton-up Euston to Wolverhampton train for a hundred

The anonymous intercity kitty.

Tibs, labelled for
the return journey
to Preston.

*Padding out of a
carriage at Euston,
she was caught by
a porter who
examined the
address on her
collar.*

and twenty miles before his miaows were heard by passengers getting off at Sandwell and Dudley station. Frozen with fear, he was plucked to safety – and promptly adopted by British Rail worker Len Johnson.

When Tibs discovered she was pregnant, she hopped on board a London-bound train – as a few ladies in similar circumstances have been wont to do. Padding out of a carriage at Euston, she was caught by a porter who examined the address on her collar. Tibs was, in fact, the station cat at Preston, in gross dereliction of her duty. With a new prominent, proper label round her neck, Tibs was despatched home in the hope that she wouldn't get any more ideas above her station.

It can be rather a different story for "accompanied" cats, as Londoner Neville Braybrooke pointed out in a letter to *The Times*. Referring to an earlier report in the paper that "a mouse can apparently travel free by train", he complained at a lack of consistency in British Rail's approach to travelling cats.

"During the past fifteen years, I have travelled over a good deal of Southern England with three different Siamese cats. On occasion the ticket collectors on British Rail have argued that since my cat was wearing a collar and on a lead, I must pay a dog's fare (which is the same as a child's). Others have said that I need only pay by weight – usually only a matter of a few shillings. Some guards have completely ignored the idea of any sum being involved at all. My happiest memory is of the Waterloo run. When the restaurant car attendant came to my compartment to announce the first service of luncheon, he saw the cat on my lap and said, 'Obviously sir, you can't go.' But ten minutes later he was back with a tray with two plates of chicken. 'One for the cat and one for the master,' he said, handing them over – and then added: 'No charge. With the compliments of British Rail.'"

Ship owners appear just as reluctant to levy charges – even though their journeys are somewhat longer. A stowaway cat spent six weeks without food in a sealed, stainless steel container during a thirteen-thousand-mile voyage to Australia. His only companion was a brand-new Mercedes car; and a customs officer in Adelaide said the cat had only survived by licking the condensation off the metal walls. Animals lovers donated seven hundred pounds for quarantine care.

Factory workers in a leather factory at Yeovil in Somerset also dipped into their pockets to pay quarantine fees. They wanted to adopt a Siamese cat which crept into a wooden chest full of skins at a port in Saudi Arabia, and survived there for four weeks until the Yeovil workers prised open the crate.

Another cat, Lucky, withstood nine weeks without food or water when he was sealed inside a container of antiques being shipped out to Texas dealer Gary Fingleman. Thanks to a prompt offer from British Caledonian, within twenty-four hours he was jetting back to the Morecambe home of his relieved owner, Linda Sinclair.

While most high-mileage cats end up trapped by their own indefatigable curiosity, a few land in trouble through sheer laziness. Tiger took a catnap in a wooden

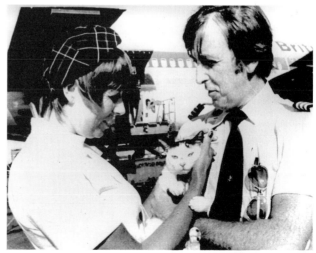

Lucky finds that this time it is British Caledonian that takes good care of you.

crate at a British Army base at Bielefeld in West Germany – and ended up in Northern Ireland. His owner, civil servant Wendy Martin, couldn't afford the two-hundred-pound quarantine bill, and Tiger was about to be put down when some Ulster cat lovers clubbed together to meet his costs.

Fatso, a champion mouse-catcher, didn't expect that when she curled up to go to sleep under a dust-cover on a comfortable-looking chair she would wake up in Jersey, one hundred and fifty miles away. But the manager of the Brewer and Turnbull warehouse in Newhaven, Sussex, was so pleased to hear she had been found safe and well that he paid the thirty shillings (it was 1968!) to fly Fatso back to Gatwick – where she was even collected by the company car.

Fatso back on home territory after her round trip to the Channel Islands.

Management consultant Roy McMillan only discovered *his* stowaway when he checked into his Geneva hotel room after flying in from London. "I'd started to unpack and was in the bathroom when I suddenly saw a kitten in the mirror. It was one hell of a shock when I realised it was my pet cat Timmy." He had apparently hitched a lift inside Roy's suit carrier – and had survived the ninety-minute journey from Heathrow in the unpressurised hold. "I kept him in my hotel room overnight," said Roy, "but the next day I had a meeting. I had no choice but to take Timmy along with me – much to the amusement of my clients." Rather than see the kitten have to go through British quarantine regulations, Roy found some friends in Germany prepared to give him a home.

Felix, a four-year-old tortoiseshell, was found starving in the hold of a Pan-Am jumbo at Heathrow airport in 1988. Her owner, US Air Force officer Bill Kubecki, was traced to America, and politely informed the airline that Felix had boarded the flight in West Germany almost a month earlier. Since squeezing out of her box in the hold she had successfully stowed away as the plane made sixty-four flights across three continents clocking up one hundred and eighty thousand miles – the equivalent of jetting round the world seven times. She had touched down in Los Angeles, Washington, New York, San Francisco and Miami – from where she took a quick trip to St Maarten in the Caribbean and Nassau in the Bahamas. Then she took in Rio de Janeiro, São Paulo, Buenos Aires, Quito and Santiago. In Europe she visited Frankfurt, Paris, Zürich, Rome and London; and even went to the Saudi Arabian capital Riyadh, as well as India. Felix survived – like others before her – by lapping condensation from the hold's walls, and was near death when rescued. A first-class flight home to America in the arms of hostess Jane Ford made her feel a lot better.

Felix receives the first-class attention of air-hostess Jane Ford.

Nine years earlier, a cat whose collar tag gave him the splendid name of Wanton Bacon went missing on the Pacific island of Guam, and was found in the hold of another Pan Am jumbo at London Airport. The only way he could have done that was by changing planes in Washington. An airline official speculated that Wanton Bacon must have walked across the tarmac and jumped on a flight to Washington where he got out to stretch his paws, taking the opportunity to transfer to the hold of a London-bound plane.

In 1953, Gingernut, Gingersnap, Cheeky and Gingerbread depended on human help when they boarded ship in South Africa for the six-thousand-mile voyage to England. All four were stowaways, aided and abetted by fanatical cat lover Miss Violet Gregorowski. Two of her charges escaped – earning her a reprimand from the

The only way he could have done that was by changing planes in Washington.

captain. But no-one knew about the other two until they all passed through Customs in London. This time the punishment was a twenty pound fine with ten pounds costs – plus, of course, the expense of keeping the cats in quarantine for six months.

Johnno, the stowaway on the *Queen Mary*, in the arms of a fellow passenger.

The crew of the *Queen Mary* found it easy enough to raise funds for such a worthy cause. Forty-five pounds of quarantine cash was raised from a whip-round organised by butcher John Hall on discovering in mid-Atlantic that they had an extra passenger – a kitten called Johnno.

But possibly the prize for the most daring feline journey – as well as the most unlikely – goes to Guiton and Puce. They ended up sailing on a wooden raft on a small lake in Pet's Corner – a part of the Duke and Duchess of Bedford's Woburn Abbey. It was but a pale shadow of the real thing. A year before – with a full-scale version of the raft, *L'Egaré II* – they'd crossed the Atlantic.

A stately home for long-distance travellers Guiton and Puce.

CARETAKER CATS

Seldom can a homeless cat have acquired a more dangerous home – and seldom can he have relished it more! Minstrel was the resident cat at the Metropolitan Police Dog Training Centre at Keston in Kent. For more than ten years, one of his jobs was to stroll casually – some might say provocatively – past the German Shepherd police dogs during their passing-out parade. Showing the ultimate confidence in the quality of their training, he didn't so much run the gauntlet as walk it, strolling with contemptuous disdain the full length of the line-up, and barely glancing at the twenty-two pairs of steely eyes boring into his black and white fur. *He* knew that *they* knew the trouble they would get into if they dared to break ranks – and took full advantage of a rare feline opportunity to assert supremacy over the sworn enemy. Kennel maid Val Andrews said that Minstrel "had settled in well. The dogs have a deep respect for him."

Minstrel provides the ultimate test.

Certainly, over the years, there has been no shortage of respect for cats that have publicly taken over great public institutions, places and occasions. If only they could speak, what tales they might tell; what political secrets could they divulge from eavesdropping on the gossip in the drawing rooms of power?

In 1873, the magazine *Punch* encapsulated the heights to which cats might aspire in a drawing by Du Maurier of ten serious gentlemen engrossed in a conspiracy to feed a kitten in a London club. Underneath was the caption "Election of an Honorary Member".

Put a cat among the bureaucrats, and they will have no trouble expanding their pen-pushing to embrace it. In 1921, the Accounts House Journal of the Director General for Defence – *In The Picture* – reproduced a quite splendid exchange of memoranda between senior naval officers and civil servants working in the Admiralty. *The Times* summed it up thus:

"Once upon a time, a hungry cat lived in an Admiralty office. He was hungry because he had to live on one shilling a week – all the cheeseparing Accountant General's office would allow him. The mouse-catcher's keeper, a kindly minor bureaucrat, applied for a bigger allowance. The Financial Secretary to the Admiralty thought that an extra sixpence a week would not bring the taxpayers out onto the streets. The First Lord, a cautious man, sent out a magisterial memorandum. It was incumbent on all good citizens to

The mouse-catcher's keeper applied for a bigger allowance.

practise frugality. It would be detrimental to the Admiralty to confer a bonus on its own cat unless special circumstances – such as an increase in family – could be adduced to support the claim. Memoranda proliferated. A Permanent Under-Secretary lauded the First Lord for sending copies of his dictum to every member of the Admiralty Board. He quoted Samuel Pepys: 'Not even a cat should swing in the Navy Office, but he [the First Lord] should know of it.' A wag, thought to be the shrewd Third Sea Lord, suggested a system of 'short-time' working for the cat, to avoid extra cost. Another wag – possibly the Second Sea Lord – unfeelingly called the cat a 'weapon', and said that, anyway, chemical warfare made cats obsolete as mousecatchers. This line of thought was icily greeted by the aforementioned Financial Secretary who had a feeling for the macabre. He said the use of poison gases, however attractive in principle, might lead to even greater expenditure owing to claims for compensation from the dependants of ex-members of the Admiralty staff. He formally proposed the sixpence increase. The First Lord now threw caution to the winds in favour of 'considerations of humanity.' The sixpence was sanctioned, and the cat lived happily – certainly replete – ever after."

Annoyingly, cats have a tendency to remain blithely unmoved by the extraordinary fuss that people often make on their behalf. At the same time, their very casualness has an ability to upstage even the most formal of occasions. They are no respecters of

An uninvited guest enjoys the Windsor pageantry.

ceremony. In 1966, a black and white stray eased herself onto a few front pages by gatecrashing the annual Service for the Order of the Garter, held in St George's Chapel at Windsor. As the Horse Guards in all their finery lined the imposing stone steps, the moggy settled down in pole position to survey members of the Royal Family passing just a few whisker-lengths away.

Back in February 1939, the auxiliary firemen of the town of Crosby were lined up in a guard of honour, waiting to be inspected by Lancashire's Chief Constable. To the delight of a waiting photographer, two black cats beat him to it – one patrolling down the line at a regal distance, while the other went for a close inspection of the firemen's boots.

Then there was Mike, a heavily bewhiskered cat who assisted in keeping the main gate of the British Museum from February 1909 to January 1929. Recording his long tenure with precise detail, the *Illustrated London News* pointed out Mike's long friendship with the archaeologist and writer, Sir Ernest A. Wallis Budge, who waxed eloquently

The moggy settled down in pole position to survey members of the Royal Family.

about his prowess. So famous did Mike become that "articles on him were published in the evening papers, and poems were written in his memory".

In 1957 there was much talk of a ghostly creature seen patrolling the rooftops of the Tower of London. It turned out to be a long-haired white cat, Snowy, newly-ensconced feline guardian of the Tower, going on his nightly rounds.

Hypo, adopted as mascot of the 406th General Hospital in

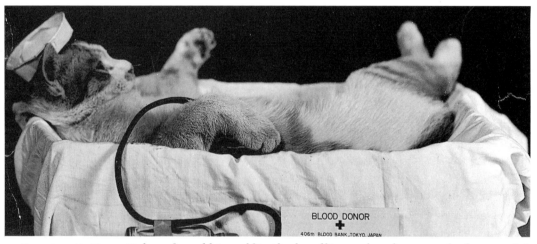

BLOOD DONOR
406th BLOOD BANK, TOKYO, JAPAN

Hypo does his bit
for the US Navy.

Tokyo, found himself in the headlines when he was asked to model for a blood donor advertisement. Although he was unable to give blood himself, his unlikely picture drew rapid attention to the urgent need for 2,800,000 pints of blood to replenish stocks for the armed services. Devised and published by the US Navy, it had millions of Americans flocking to Red Cross Chapters or Blood Donor Centres across the USA.

There was much talk of a ghostly creature seen patrolling the rooftops of the Tower of London.

Places of power to which cats have been drawn include the British Embassy in Moscow, where Carrington (named after the then British Foreign Secretary) ruled the roost; the City of London, which once boasted a prize mouser called Tosh, the pet of the River Police; and Lloyd's of

118

London, whose recent troubles have not forced any redundancies amongst the latest in a long line of syndicate cats. In 1952, the Stock Exchange invested in a cat called Tibs, to replace the famous Minnie, who, sadly, collected her final dividends as she attempted to cross Throgmorton Street against some unexpectedly fast traffic.

Peter, the Home Office cat, died in March 1964 after stalking mice through the building's two hundred rooms and numerous corridors for sixteen years. Speeding to fill his pawmarks came Peta, a Manx cat which the Isle of Man government ceremonially presented to the then Home Secretary, Henry Brooke. An enthusiastic cat-lover, he was reported to have tickled her under the whiskers, whispering "Kaniss Theshoo", which is Manx for "How Are You". Peta, however, seemed rather more interested in the Treasury's decision to celebrate her arrival by doubling the official government cat allowance to five shillings a week. But, sadly, such spirited decisions are no more. Succumbing to the new technological age, Home Office cats have now been phased out in favour of mousetraps.

Top
Carrington – Our Cat in Moscow.
Above
Peta takes over at the Home Office.

Downing Street is different. No Prime Minister wishing to be re-elected would be seen to turn away a cat. Cats know this – and are deeply appreciative that the security gates recently erected at the entrance to Downing Street still allow them to come and go without any tiresome police checks. To settle down in the prime basket in the country is still regarded as the peak of every stray's ambition. A black kitten struck lucky when he happened to turn up on Number Ten's doorstep on the very day of Winston Churchill's speech to the 1953 Conservative Conference at Margate. Such timing and symbolism earned him an instant home – where he could perhaps browse over sketches of the ginger tom that was a previous Churchillian favourite. A delightful series of cat portraits was drawn for Mrs Churchill by none other than Sir William Nicholson. But undoubtedly the most famous Downing Street cat was Wilberforce, who arrived in 1973 and, over the next fifteen years, had the honour of being regularly tickled by no fewer than four Prime Ministers – Edward Heath, Harold Wilson, James Callaghan and Margaret Thatcher. Rescued by the Hounslow RSPCA when he was just a kitten, this tabby and white shorthaired cat snaffled enough prawns from official receptions to weigh in eventually at a comfortable twenty-one pounds. Needless to say, he outlasted the passing attentions of the Wilson labrador, Paddy, and of Budget, Sir Geoffrey Howe's Jack Russell terrier from the Chancellor's residence next door. Such was Wilberforce's fame that when he died, virtually the whole of Fleet Street waxed lyrical in tribute. *Cat World* described how "the best mouser in Britain died peacefully in his sleep on 19 May 1988". Political editor, Julia Langdon, reported that "tributes from all four Prime Ministers who had known and loved him flowed into the *Daily Mirror* last night from across the world". She revealed that only one person would *not* lament the passing of Wilberforce – and that was Mrs Thatcher's Press Secretary, Bernard Ingham. The reason? "Wilberforce habitually slept on Mr Ingham's desk – and gave him asthma."

Wilberforce on patrol in Downing Street.

Wilberforce had the honour of being regularly tickled by no fewer than four Prime Ministers.

News of the vacancy at Number Ten spread like wildfire amongst London's strays. After a suitably respectful period of time had elapsed, a ferocious black and white tom walked in off the street and volunteered his services to the Cabinet Office. Staff named him Humphrey, after the Cabinet Secretary Sir Humphrey Appleby in the BBC TV series *Yes, Prime Minister*; and he became a particular favourite with the real Cabinet Secretary, Sir Robin Butler, who put him officially on the staff list, and, according to the *Daily Mail*, even took out a private Pet Plan health insurance policy covering Humphrey for £1,000 of vets fees, £750 for accidental damage, and an astonishing one million pounds for third-party liability.

American President Theodore Roosevelt would have approved – he was potty about cats, the most famous being Slippers, a grey cat that

Humphrey, the new man at Number Ten.

became famous because it allegedly had "extra toes". But after Slippers died, the White House denied itself a cat for almost sixty years – until pressure from the young daughters of more recent Presidents – Caroline Kennedy, Susan Ford and Amy Carter – forced a change of heart.

If a cat has an urgent need of fame, it has but to hang out in a well-known literary haunt, and just lounge around hoping to be discovered. A white and marmalade moggy called Hamlet hit the jackpot when he strolled into New York's Algonquin Hotel and stayed for twelve years. Feted by visiting actors and writers alike, the peak of his career came with the publication of Val Schnaffner's book *The Algonquin Cat*. And when Hamlet died, the London *Times* ran an obituary – albeit in its gossip column – reporting that "first signs that something might be wrong were spotted a few days ago when he took refuge under a sofa in the lobby and was barely able to acknowledge the greeting of Anthony Andrews and other members of a visiting party from *Brideshead Revisited*, currently in New York for the American launch of the series." Revealing that he died of kidney failure in a New York veterinary hospital, *The Times* concluded that "Hamlet's familiar face at the entrance to the crowded and hospitable lobby will be much missed."

London's Savoy Hotel hit on a way of ensuring that *its* cat never went missing, whatever the reason. For sixty-five years, a splendid black wooden sculpture of Kaspar has been on hand to set at ease the minds of those who might be superstitious about taking part in

A convenient
resting-place in
the Père Lachaise
cemetery.

a private dinner party consisting of thirteen guests. Impeccably carved by Basil Ionides, the Black Cat's job is to be the fourteenth guest.

Where would cats go if there were no people for them to comfort and help? One macabre answer is the abandoned graves of Paris. In the Père Lachaise cemetery, cats at one time established a small city of their own, living and multiplying amidst the tombstones and deserted vaults. In 1990, the *Sunday Telegraph* reported a tomcat in residence in London's Highgate Cemetery. "A ginger stray of uncertain age, he spends much of his time sitting on top of an old tomb containing the ashes of the English philosopher Herbert Spencer (1820–1903). What he stares at is Marx's tomb, which is on the other side of a pebbled path just opposite his perch." It may well have been the last catcall for communism!

Sensible cats make better use of their time. One turned up at Lord's cricket gound in 1979 for a close look at the Australian fast bowler Jeff Thomson practising at the nets on the eve of the Second Test. While a tiny ginger kitten became a devotee of another spectator sport – the traffic jams in London's Blackwall Tunnel. In 1983, maintenance staff cleaning out the tunnel found "Blackwall", as he was rather obviously named, hiding behind a fire hydrant.

Jeff Thomson and
friend at Lord's.

The only way he could have got there was by jumping out, or being thrown out, of a passing car. Gently revived in the control room above the tunnel entrance, he looked at his new surroundings and decided to stay. Growing into a huge, friendly tom, he based himself in the maintenance areas

above the tunnel entrance, with regular forays into an adjacent lorry park. He doesn't seem to mind the noise and exhaust fumes that inevitably fill the air as he dodges the traffic. But what he really likes best are his regular cleaning sessions when staff run a vacuum cleaner over his nooks and crannies to remove the dirt!

No need for that at Britain's major film studios in 1937, when production of the film *Lancashire Luck* was briefly interrupted by the Pinewood studio cat giving birth to ten kittens. As the father was the neighbouring Denham studio cat, it was clear they had decided that patrolling the huge film lots was too big a job for just two moggies. The studios arranged an immediate photocall, and the film's star, actress Wendy Hiller, had no complaints about being upstaged ten times.

Some cats have been known to tread the boards themselves – accidentally, of course, and usually as a result of a momentary neglect of their caretaker duties in the theatres of London's West End. Doyen of

Wendy Hiller with the new arrivals at Denham studios.

them all is Beerbohm, a perpetually inquisitive and aristocratic tabby who gives the impression of owning the Globe Theatre on Shaftesbury Avenue. Indeed, his framed photograph hangs in the foyer. A refugee from Her Majesty's Theatre, he was named after its great actor-manager, Herbert Beerbohm Tree, who would not have approved of his habit of interrupting productions with surprise appearances. The *Mail On Sunday* paid lavish tribute to him, recalling how he "invariably stole the scene and caused rifts among the players, testing their ad-libbing skills to the full. In a classroom scene in *Daisy Pulls It Off* the headmistress coolly instructed one of the pupils to 'remove that cat'. And when the stage was covered with twenty tons of sand and flagstones for *The House of Bernard*

Beerbohm mistook it for a giant litter tray and indulged in a night of frenzied activity.

Alba, Beerbohm mistook it for a giant litter tray and indulged in a night of frenzied activity which the theatre staff are still trying to forget." He once ate the feathers off Beryl Reid's hat. But his greatest culinary exploit came when he polished off eighty pounds worth of stuffed birds decorating the set of a play about Dr Livingstone.

The Everyman Cinema in Hampstead once boasted five cats, fond of warming themselves on the projection equipment. *The Magazine* recorded that "although they are great favourites at the Kid's Cinema Club on a Saturday morning, they have been barred from the auditorium during the rest of the week after one of them leapt unexpectedly into a woman's lap during a showing of *Psycho*."

Through it all, caretaker cats live a lonely existence, often deprived of human company for long periods at a time. The actress Beryl Reid summed up their plight when explaining why she took the Lyric Theatre's cat, Fleur, home with her at night. "It's not just a question of feeding cats," she said. "They need looking at."

CATS' HOME COMFORTS

"Mrs Goodman's Hospital For Cats, New York" was the caption; the date, July 1875. With the help of a delightful sketch by Beryham, the *Illustrated Sporting and Dramatic News* introduced its readers to the pioneering work of an American cat lover. By 1910, *The Sphere* was devoting a full-page spread to a London institution "devoted solely to cats". A horse-drawn van patrolled the streets of the city boldly advertising "A Home For Lost And Starving Cats" at 36-42 Ferdinand Street, Camden Town. The service, promised the sign, was "free to the poor", with "no gratuities allowed". A lady, dressed rather formally as a nurse, supervised the cats' feeding time. A serious-looking gentleman was shown binding a moggy's injured leg, and even extracting a cat's tooth.

The word spread, and in 1935 came evidence of a new, improved French version. The *Illustrated London News* reported on a Cats' Home on the Boulevard Berthier in Paris, set up at the initiative of Mme du Gast, President of the French Society for the Protection of Animals. "On the first storey of the building is a lofty room with the entry closed by a grill. Here some twenty she-cats are accommodated (tom-cats, it should be noted, have a similar hotel at Gennevilliers). Round the room are set little boxes which serve as beds. On the ground are saucers filled with water or food – which is principally meat or rice. The window opens

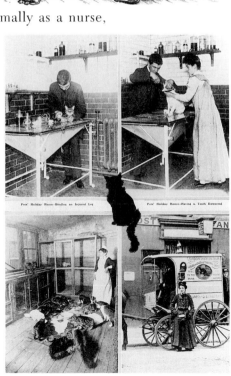

Pets' Holiday Home.—Binding an Injured Leg

Pets' Holiday Home.—Having a Tooth Extracted

onto a terrace, also enclosed with a grill. The animals have a means of making their way down into the garden, where a larger cage enables them to disport themselves at greater liberty: a trapdoor in the wall opens, revealing a long tunnel of netting which leads down to the ground at a steep angle. This is called the toboggan, and the cats eagerly make use of it to get into the open air." And just in case it was raining, Mme du Gast had designed an indoor "cat walk" leading up to and across the mantelpiece, and (in a forerunner of the modern rope-covered scratching-post) installed a dining

A MODEL HOME FOR LOST CATS IN PARIS.

A HOME FOR LOST CATS IN PARIS WHICH MAKES SPECIAL PROVISION FOR THE EXERCISE AND RECREATION OF ITS INMATES: THE WIRE-ENCLOSED "TOBOGGAN" USED BY THE CATS WHEN GOING DOWN FROM THEIR DWELLING-ROOM ON THE FIRST FLOOR TO THEIR EXERCISE CAGE IN THE GARDEN.

LOUNGE, BEDROOM AND DINING-ROOM IN ONE IN A CATS' "HOTEL DE LUXE": AN APARTMENT IN THE ESTABLISHMENT IN THE BOULEVARD BERTHIER FITTED OUT WITH SLEEPING BOXES, EATING AND DRINKING BOWLS, AND A "WALK" OVER THE MANTELPIECE; TABLE-LEGS BEING SPECIALLY PROVIDED FOR SHARPENING CLAWS ON!

"Warm, purified air" was guaranteed in all sixty rooms, and entertainment was provided by the wireless!

table just so that the cats could sharpen their claws on its legs.

Come 1953, and Edith Allen was advertising a hotel for cats at Hampton in Middlesex – a place where they could be left while their owners went on holiday. "Warm, purified air" was guaranteed in all sixty rooms, and entertainment was provided by the wireless! According to Miss Allen, it soothed the cats, and stopped them fretting or disturbing each other. The feeding free-for-all of the 1910 London home had been abandoned in favour of personalised room service. Each cat had meals served in its own room – on a numbered dish. Several veterinary surgeons, a dietician and a bacteriologist were on twenty-four-hour call. And, just in case all that should fail to please, owners were encouraged to send their pets postcards to "cheer them up" while they were away.

Amsterdam's canal-side cats' home.

You could only improve on that by offering rooms "right on the waterfront". Henrietta van Weelde did just that with her floating residence on the Singel, one of Amsterdam's canals. Rooms opened out onto a fenced-off veranda, so that the cats saunter along for their afternoon constitutional in the sun.

The ultimate delight for cats must be a hotel where they can come and go as they please. Millicent Grover opened one in the Devon resort of Torbay. Situated "in a quiet, shady nook in the cliffs, overlooking the sea", each cat had a cubicle five feet long, two feet wide and six feet high, complete with central heating and its own windows and balconies. Special diets were catered for – and they had more than their share of eccentrics. One cat needed an alarm

One cat needed an alarm clock to wake it, and expected an instant saucer of milk as it lifted itself from its slumbers.

Toffee opens his
account.

She started a "meals on wheels" service, using her scooter to deliver tasty morsels to temporarily abandoned moggies!

More satisfied
customers for
Beryl Saunders.

clock to wake it, and expected an instant saucer of milk as it lifted itself from its slumbers. Another had to be surrounded by toys – especially dolls – before it would settle down to sleep. Owners could relax on holiday happy in the knowledge that there was an excellent sick bay, and that every cat was guaranteed "a daily three-minute cuddle to maintain family togetherness".

For one guest, that was a long-term undertaking. When seventeen-year-old Toffee checked in, it was for life! His owners, the Loftus family, decided to emigrate to Australia, but felt that the long journey would be too much of an upheaval for a cat of Toffee's years. So they deposited enough money for him in the local bank to pay his hotel bills for the rest of his days. That made Toffee probably the only cat in Britain to have his own bank account.

But what about those cats who refuse to leave home when their owners disappear on holiday – no matter how luxurious the alternative accommodation on offer might be? Beryl Saunders had the answer to that one – in Bournemouth at least. In 1959 she started a "meals on wheels" service, using her scooter to deliver tasty morsels to any temporarily abandoned moggies!

For most cats, there is no substitute for home – which, to them, is simply the basket or cushion on the warm side of the cat-flap. But a few end up with something much

128

grander. There is no particular reason why cats should prefer their own small houses, in some cases complete with chimneys. But such delightful extravagances certainly keep their owners happy. Londoner Mrs C. Davey was in the news in 1957 when she provided her cat Whisky with his own small cottage in her garden. And by 1964, more than sixty unwanted cats were living in specially designed miniature chalets at the Wood Green Animal Shelter near Royston in Hertfordshire – with regular meals delivered almost to their doors by Superintendent Sidney Smith. It was only a matter of time before houses became widely available to cats everywhere! In 1985, a firm in Newcastle-Upon-Tyne began marketing a "Cat Villa" – a cardboard box printed to look like a thatched cottage,

Mealtime at Wood Green.

Window seat for Tibby.

with cut-out doors and windows. Not a bad buy for just two pounds! A *Sunday Times* survey showed that three out of four cats preferred it – while the fourth climbed on the roof.

Tibby and Smurf were more used to climbing into their *mobile* home. Whenever Louis and Alice Addy left their Leeds house to go touring on a tandem, their cats tagged along too – in a purpose-built sidecar. In 1980 they were quite an attraction. The "Pussy Pullman" even made a trip from North Wales across England to Bridlington to raise cash for a hospital charity.

It was at about the same time that Ronald McGriff hit the streets in New

Ronald McGriff stops the traffic on West 59th Street.

York, cycling along at the head of his "cat train" – complete with a couple of open carriages for his six pets. Not all of them took the opportunity to show how lazy they were. Some rode; some ran, preferring to pad along as feline outriders. New York being New York, nobody turned a hair!

Some cats just don't appreciate how lucky they are to have a home. In 1955, a certain Miss Arminella actually sold her home and possessions so she could go on looking after sixty strays. First to go was Chase Lodge, where she had lived with her parents until they died. And Miss Arminella moved, with her belongings and cats, into a little room above the stables. Then, piece by piece, she had to sell the valuable furniture and carpets to pay the fish and meat bills for her growing family. As word got round that she would never turn a cat away, people started leaving animals on her doorstep. Soon, all that was left were bare boards and one tallboy. Then the Cats' Protection League came galloping to the rescue, taking over the entire establishment – and Miss Arminella. To stay with her cats, she took on the job of warden in the house she had once owned.

As word got round that she would never turn a cat away, people started leaving animals on her doorstep.

The local council at Northleach in Gloucestershire weren't nearly so tolerant with Christine Hayley and her thirteen cats. They ordered her to give up eleven of them –' and said she would have to leave her two-bedroomed council house if she did not.

Sylvia Phillips could have reassured them that having a household of cats doesn't mean living "in smelly squalor". She had ninety-one of them – in a rambling ten-room house standing in half an acre at Headingley in Leeds – and reckons she knows every one by name. It all began twenty years earlier when she took pity on a stray, and let it join the two Siamese who then ruled the roost. "Gradually," said Sylvia, "I acquired more and more." Her tribe of cats drink eight pints of milk a day to wash down meals of minced beef, vitamins and cat food. She said that her unmarried son, George, who lives with her "is not particularly mad about cats, but helps with the washing up". That works out at ninety-one plates twice a day! To say nothing of emptying the litter trays!

But the "Award For The Most Cats Under One Roof" must go to John Wright, a Canadian decorator, and his wife Donna. In 1988 they were the undisputed winners of a newspaper competition with that very title. Having started taking in strays twenty years earlier, they ended up caring for no fewer than one hundred and sixty-eight cats in their three-bedroom house.

They ended up caring for no fewer than one hundred and sixty-eight cats in their three-bedroom house.

Only one person seems in the running to beat that target – Saudi Sheik Mohammed al-Fassi. Appalled at learning that some humane groups have cats put down if their owners aren't found, he has turned his two-million-pound bayfront mansion in Miami into a home for stray cats. When last interviewed, he had over a hundred cats sharing seven rooms of their own in one of the most expensive houses in Florida. A private vet, nurses and a permanent staff of nine are employed to look after them. The man who paid to have ten doomed cats

flown to his home from New Jersey made this appeal to the American public: "If you are thinking of having your cat put down, please don't. Send it to me instead. I feel it is my responsibility to free all cats."

Terry Moore wants to save cats too. But only exotic and rare wildcats. In 1990, the *Daily Mail* tracked him down to his farm in leafy Hertfordshire, where he and his wife Judith keep thirty-five animals that you wouldn't normally find in front of the average family hearth. There are seven pure-bred jungle cats, the species thought to be the ancestors of all our domestic cats; nine bobcats; two lynxes; three Scottish wildcats; four leopard or Bengal cats; two Indian desert cats; and eight Geoffroy's, who look like dainty ocelot kittens, and produce only one offspring a year.

> *"A delectable little Geoffroy's cat from South America, his face alive with interest, hobbles to meet us on three legs."*

In fact, at the Cat Survival Trust – the charity which the Moores gave up their Hi-Fi business to run – they have bred twenty-four Geoffroy's, "more than all the zoos in Europe put together". Reporter June Southworth recalled meeting one who arrived a different way. "A delectable little Geoffroy's cat from South America, his face alive with interest, hobbles to meet us on three legs. He came from a zoo where he had made an unlucky escape into the jaws of the jaguar next door. In the wild the jaguar would have eaten him." But Terry's favourite is one particular jungle cat called JCB. He explained why: "He came from a zoo and was exceedingly wild. Whatever we did to try to calm him, he kept striking out. We couldn't understand it. We suddenly noticed that he was bumping into things. We put his food into a plastic bag and placed it down in front of him – *and he didn't see it* . We realised he was blind. It had been caused when the zoo had given him an overdose of an antibiotic that has now been withdrawn. With love and care he's become totally confident with people. He's a real softie now because he's happy and safe."

CAT HEROES

What makes a cat a hero? Is it an act of bravery? Or a natural exercising of a sixth sense which humans interpret as a life-saving warning? Or perhaps devotion over and beyond the call of duty, often pushing natural instincts to one side? The world's media have not been slow to find "heroes" in all three categories.

She happily shared her food with the sparrow, and gently played with it, showing no hostile intentions at all.

When Mr and Mrs Polak of Miami, Florida, found a young, abandoned sparrow, they took it in to keep it out of the way of neighbourhood cats, and gave it a cage in which to recover. They were as amazed as anyone when their cat, Kitty Wimple, far from being hostile, started showing a friendly interest. She happily shared her food with the sparrow, and gently played with it,

Kitty Wimple goes visiting.

showing no hostile intentions at all. Before long, Kitty Wimple couldn't stand seeing her feathered friend back in its cage – and took every opportunity to try to "break in" to entice it out to play.

In 1957, an American National Cat Food Camp awarded a heroine's medal to Minnie, a Siamese from Boston, who decided not to make a meal of a pigeon with a broken leg. Instead, she brought it home to her owner, Joseph Menex, who saved its life.

No medals – only publicity – for the owl and the pussycat who abandoned the nursery rhyme to strike up a working relationship on land – in Wallingford, near Oxford, to be precise. John Holmes's kitten, Felix, bounced, stalked and tentatively patted Oscar the owl, who, remaining completely

unruffled by it all, just blinked patiently.

Two observant boys who pulled two half-frozen puppies from certain death in an icy pond on London's Clapham Common can hardly have guessed that a cat would come to the rescue too. Instead of raising her hackles, she promptly adopted the two waifs, encouraging them to share her basket

Top Felix examines Oscar with an exploratory paw. **Above** Mum shows her kitten and her adopted puppies what to do with a bowl of milk.

and bowl with her own somewhat bemused kitten.

A family in the German city of Hamburg found a tiny, frightened baby hedgehog curled into a spiny ball in their back garden. Weighing no more than five ounces, it could barely open its eyes – and was promptly adopted by the family cat, Liescha, presumably as a substitute for two of her kittens who had just been found new homes. Another German cat overcame her natural aversion to hedgehogs when she was asked to foster three babies who had been

found squatting beside their dead mother on a farm near Alt-Ötting. Her mothering instincts were so strong that she allowed them to compete with her own kittens in the regular jostle for milk from her belly.

A Danish cat caused a zoological sensation when it fostered a squirrel. Two children were out looking for birds' nests when, in one of them, they found eight newborn squirrels. Six of them happily took to bottle feeding, but the other two refused. So they were put in a basket with a cat who

Prickly competition for one hungry kitten.

had just had kittens. When last hitting the headlines, they were reported to be growing up as one big happy family.

A Danish cat caused a zoological sensation when it fostered a squirrel.

Duchesse, a white madame of a cat, who lived in St Jean-St Maurice in the Loire region, was distraught when all her kittens were given away soon after they were born. So she jumped at the chance to foster nine baby rabbits. Her motherly love – and milk – saved them all from certain death.

The Danish foster-mother keeps a watchful eye on her assorted young.

If cats are heroes, padding to the rescue in the animal world, it is hardly surprising that they can appear as heroes to humans as well! The *Daily Star* reported how "Fluffy the Persian saved the life of a new-born baby abandoned on a freezing night." Her owner, Margaret Weir, a nurse at an old people's home in Nottingham, was puzzled when Fluffy refused to come in after her evening prowl. She sat pointedly on the doorstep, and then wandered off into the bushes. Margaret

followed – to find Fluffy sitting miaowing beside a bundle. "I thought it was just a pile of rubbish," she said. "But when I looked closer I saw a hand. Then I heard a child whimpering. She was struggling, and I took her in." The baby girl – a healthy seven pounds eight ounces – quickly recovered at Queen's medical centre. A hunt went on for the mother who abandoned her – while appropriate praise was lavished on the cat, who didn't.

The American magazine *Cat Fancy* published a letter from Kelli A. Kinsman of Dracut, Massachusetts, recounting how her half-Siamese cat had saved her from an attack. "One day when I was five months pregnant, I was returning to our sliding glass door after feeding the birds. Just as I was starting to re-enter our home, a tall, tan dog came out of nowhere and leapt at me, knocking me down against the glass. Luckily I had left the door open a few inches when I went out. My cat, Flash, flew out the door, wrapped himself around the dog's throat and proceeded to bring his front paws up and scratch at the dog's eyes. The dog ran yelping away, while little eight-and-a-half pound Flash stood hissing at its rapidly retreating back."

At nineteen pounds, Misty, a Turkish Angora Blue, used the warmth of her weight to save the life of senior citizen Roger Sear. It happened during a particularly bitter winter, when the wall-mounted heater that Roger counted on to heat his room developed a fault in the middle of the night. He woke at four in the morning to find the glass of water beside his bed was frozen solid, and he had, not surprisingly, developed hypothermia. "I was," he said, "numb with cold and losing coherent thought. I tried to reach the bell beside my bed, but I couldn't move. Then I felt something heavy and furry pressing against my neck and shoulders. Misty was licking me and purring. It was like having a hot-water bottle on my chest. I began to feel warm." Roger continued "I know it's dangerous to switch on an electric blanket when you're in bed, but I decided to risk it – I was feeling desperate. Then I dropped the cable – and was too weak to reach it – but Misty, realising my plight, managed to grab the cable with her paws and pass it to me. Once I had begun to warm up a bit, I rang the bell to alert my wife, Peggy, and she called the doctor." The couple recalled that seven years earlier, when Misty was a kitten, and extremely ill, Peggy had nursed her back to health. The debt was repaid.

According to the *Eastern Daily Press*, Wigs the cat was hailed a hero by firemen for saving her owner's life in a house fire at Grantham in Lincolnshire. Wigs jumped onto twenty-one-year-old Julie Franklin's bed as smoke filled her room – and nudged her awake. Julie paid due tribute: "I couldn't see a thing and I could barely breathe. I would have slept on, and been suffocated in my sleep, if Wigs hadn't saved me."

> *"Misty was licking me and purring. It was like having a hot-water bottle on my chest. I began to feel warm."*

The miaowing of pet cat Tyson saved the entire Clarke family when flames from a burning chip pan engulfed their home in Middleton near Manchester. Woken by his cries, the parents, Peter and Kathleen, dashed from their bedroom choking from the fumes, and found their son Wayne semi-conscious downstairs. Fire Officer Alan Bailey told the *Manchester Evening News*, "If the cat had not raised the alarm, they would have slept on and wouldn't have stood a chance of getting out alive. Fire completely burnt out the kitchen, and caused extensive damage to the rest of the house. They have a lot to thank the cat for."

Across the years – and many countries – fire survivors talk of owing their lives to cats who raised their voices in a sound likened to a screech, a high-pitched moan, or even a baby crying! But not all such stories have happy endings. London's *Evening Standard* reported how William and Sandra Wood escaped from a fire in their mobile home in Venice, Florida. Their cat, Smokey, jumped on Sandra's stomach and alerted them to the fire. They raced to safety – but Smokey died of smoke-poisoning in the bedroom. The

Fire Chief, Joe Patek, said, "They wouldn't have made it if it hadn't been for that cat. The animal was a real hero."

In 1952, they were handing out medals for such acts of feline bravery. Film Actress Kathleen Harrison turned up at Acton Town Hall to present a Blue Cross – a sort of animal's Victoria Cross awarded by the Dumb Friends' League. Proud recipient was a tortoiseshell kitten – coincidentally also called Smokey – whose warning cries saved the lives of the Donovan family, including baby daughter Marilyn.

When cats display their heroic nature in the way they protect their young, or show exceptional dedication to their work, their feats often achieve permanent recognition. The wall of St Augustine's Church, in London's Watling Street, bears the picture of a vicar's cat called Faith – and records how she saved her kitten during the Second World War. "Normally Faith slept upstairs in the vicarage, but on 6 September 1940 she became restless and suddenly lifted her kitten out of its basket. Carrying it down three storeys, she put it in a pigeonhole in the wall where music was kept. Four times the vicar took the kitten upstairs and each time Faith brought it back. So the vicar gave orders that the pigeonhole should be cleaned and the cat's basket put there. Faith immediately settled in happily. Three days later – while the vicar

Facing Page
Smokey, the fire alarm, with his medal.

139

was out – the building was bombed. Faith sat through the whole night of bombing and fire, guarding her kitten. The roofs and masonry exploded. The house blazed. Floors fell through in front of her; fire and water and ruin were all around her. Yet she stayed steadfast and calm and waited for help. She was rescued in the early morning, while the place was still burning. Faith and her kitten were not only saved, but unhurt."

Faith sat through the whole night of bombing and fire, guarding her kitten.

Fat Albert was patently failing to live up to his name when he turned up at the Marlton Animal Hospital in New Jersey. In fact, he was pretty well on his last paws. But the nurses brought him back to such a peak of health and fitness that he became their official blood donor, helping to save many other feline lives. There are now several animal clinics in America where owners queue up so that their cats can give blood to help "victims of trauma" and other life-threatening medical conditions, from rodenticide poisoning to road accidents. At the Angell Memorial Animal Hospital in Boston, the "state-of-the-art intensive care wing" carries out three hundred life-saving transfusions every year – and needs a steady stream of pets prepared to help their fellow cats. Volunteers have to pass a comprehensive medical exam which includes testing for feline leukaemia. Those who make it through to the final selection are offered "a quiet resting area and pet treats, including a tasty and refreshing soft drink". It means that cats can now come to the rescue of cats that they haven't even met.

It means that cats can now come to the rescue of cats that they haven't even met.

Ginger, a marmalade-coloured tomcat, made such a good job of keeping down the mouse population of Salisbury Cathedral that, when he died in 1988, he was given his own hero's gravestone. On it was carved the epitaph "A Cat of Great Character". And just to

This kitten was supposed to have helped nurse the injured duckling, but from the way she's licking her lips the original caption may be misleading!

reinforce the memory of his impact on the life of the thirteenth-century Cathedral, the authorities had him immortalised in a new stained-glass window.

During the American Civil War, the troops manning an isolated fort in the Confederate South acquired a cat called Tom, whose grey coat matched their uniforms. He patrolled the fort's earthen tunnels, keeping them free of giant river rats – and was in the thick of a mighty battle between the guns of the fort and those of three new Union ironclad battleships manoeuvred into the mouth of the Ogeechee River. The South won the battle by brilliantly concealing the extent of the damage inside the fort. But there was one casualty – Tom. The magazine *Cat Fancy*, recalling the incident, admitted that Tom was an unlikely war hero, "but because he had not run away during the massive bombing by the Union ships, he was as close to a war hero as a cat could get. Later, when the Confederate commanding officer sent his report of the attack to Army headquarters, he recorded that Tom had been killed in the incident. Tom may be the only cat listed as a casualty of the Civil War.

Today, a bronze plaque stands in Fort McAllister, dedicated to the memory of Tom – the cat in grey."

Another brave ratter did manage to survive the rigours of battle. Simon, a black and white cat belonging to the captain of HMS *Amethyst*, went to war in April 1949 when the guns of Chinese communist batteries opened fire on his ship in the Yangtse River. A shell landed on the captain's cabin, killing him, wounding Simon in several places, and singeing his fur and whiskers. A shocked Simon kept his head down for a few days – until he discovered that the shelling had shaken numerous rats out of their normal hiding place. He made so many catches that they were all recorded on a list – and he carried on ratting as the ship made its legendary dash down the river to the open sea.

News of his heroism preceded him, and when the crippled *Amethyst* limped into Hong Kong, Simon found himself inundated with letters, telegrams, tins of food, and even cheques to buy cream. But, in quarantine, he pined so much for his ship-mates that no-one could save him. Simon died before he could be presented personally with a Dickin medal – but in the annals of naval history they will never forget the cat that won a posthumous "VC".

But, in quarantine, he pined so much for his ship-mates that no-one could save him.

MISCHIEVOUS AND MARAUDING MOGGIES

Through the political dining rooms of London in the 1820s echoed tales of a cat which apparently kept Members of Parliament under control even better than Mr Speaker. The writings of the diarist Thomas Creevey describe a dinner party at the home of the prominent Whig politican, and former Lord Privy Seal, Lord Holland, who helped to abolish the slave trade. It is

apparent that Lord Holland's desire to end master-and-slave relationships did not stretch to his wife's cat or their many guests. At one of Lady Holland's noted soirées Creevey met her "huge animal, which is never permitted to be out of her sight, and to whose vagaries she demands unqualified submission from all her visitors". Lord Brougham (later Lord Chancellor) was only able to keep him or her at arms length by the judicious use of snuff, and "Samuel Rogers, the poet and conversationalist, has, it seems, already sustained considerable injury in a personal affair with this animal. Luttrell has sent in a formal resignation of all further visits until this odious new favourite is dismissed from the Cabinet."

Cats that display such instinctive dislike of people - such ruthless high-handedness with friends of their master or mistress - are fortunately rare. And it may well be that the fault lay not with the cat, but in the characters or attitudes of Messrs Rogers, Luttrell *et al*. But, while domestic cats are generally noted for their placid disposition, there are a few who have risen to public prominence by unusual, outrageous or mischievous behaviour. Residents in the Hertfordshire village of Digswell once waited in dread for a ghostly

Residents waited in dread for a ghostly and erratic tapping on their doors.

and erratic tapping on their doors that woke them up in the dead of the night. Fears that burglars were about proved unfounded, but no-one could trace the source of the phantom knocking - until Mrs Elizabeth Hipgrave quietly leaned out of her bedroom window after being disturbed yet again by the ghostly marauder. There, tugging at the door-knocker with her paw, was Pussy Galore, the fat old cat from next door. The next day, when confronted with the evidence, Pussy's owner, Molly White, explained all. She had taught Pussy to knock on their door whenever she wanted to come in; but, for some reason, the Whites hadn't been hearing her recently, so Pussy had done the rounds of the village in the hope that someone would take her in from the cold.

More apologies were called for

Pussy Galore tries to attract attention.

when thirteen-year-old Tamara Oppenheimer discovered that her tabby, Elijah, had been "terrorising" part of Oxford by stealing children's teddy bears. Alison McLennan, who was only seven, arrived home to find that two of her teddies had disappeared. Discussions with neighbours revealed a trail of similarly heartbroken youngsters. Tamara realised what was happening when she found Elijah's secret hoard - not just teddies, but also wooden

dolls, toy rabbits, slippers and all manner of odds and bobs. Everyone was invited to an identity parade to reclaim their favourite toys, while Elijah looked on in sullen disgust.

Dinky admires one of his recent acquisitions.

Another klepto-maniacal cat could at least own up to more acceptable collecting habits. Dinky brought home fifteen live fish after raids on neighbours' ponds in and around Southampton - to the astonishment of his owner, Pauline Herbdige. Nine of them survived - including one he "rescued" from a frozen pond. Pauline's husband Bill reckoned that all he had to do was to train Dinky to

Spyke spots the
postman.

drop his fish straight into their pond, and he'd never have to restock it again.

Spyke took out his aggression on the local postmen. He attacked four of them as they tried to deliver letters to his owners in Bury, Lancashire. So the local sorting office put out a general warning to alert those deliverymen tempted to take a cavalier view of the "Beware of the Cat" sign hanging ominously below the letter-box. Spyke's owners, Lindsey and John Holder, insisted that it was all a terrible misunderstanding, and Spyke was only trying to protect them.

Mischief-maker Nebukadnezer made a little cat history in Norway when his antics started a fire that completely gutted the house of his owner, Ole Olsen. He was climbing the curtains when his weight pulled them down, and they fell onto an electric heater. The blaze spread rapidly, and the panic-stricken Olsen children - Kate, who was eleven, and nine-year old Vivi - managed to escape just as the roof fell in. Nebukadnezer too made good his escape - to be reunited with a family who, despite such a disaster, were simply delighted to see him alive.

His antics started a fire that completely gutted the house of his owner.

No such accidents for Sylvester the roaming tomcat. He planned his life with enviable precision, managing to keep *three* homes on the go all at the same time. His two-timing tactics only surfaced when Adele and David Latham, who had long believed they owned him, took him to the vet to be treated for a leg injury. They were stunned when the vet revealed that he had already treated the wound twice before, when Sylvester had been brought in by *other* owners. On reflection, everything fell into place. And the Lathams realised why the cat

146

they'd thought was a stray kept nipping off for a few hours every day, and often turned his nose up at their food.

Rogan, a ginger tomcat, had a more disturbing reason for being off his food. He was deeply affected by a series of apparent poltergeist disturbances at Jane Conynham's thirteenth-century cottage at Monks Eleigh, near Ipswich. "We were," said Jane, "being plagued by things moving, and strange tapping and footstep noises." So a retired clergyman, Canon John Griffin, was called in. He moved towards Rogan, saying a prayer, and then gently laid his hands on the cat in a blessing. At first Rogan shook and trembled, but slowly he became quiet and relaxed. The strange disturbances at the old cottage continued, but Rogan was much more relaxed about them.

Life returns to normal for Rogan.

A builder converting an old mill at Sudbury in Suffolk into an hotel came across the mummified body of a cat beneath some floorboards. It had apparently been buried alive three centuries earlier to ward off evil spirits, as local superstition then demanded. But its removal from the original grave produced a baffling series of disasters. Builder Arthur Kemp decided to remove the cat and store it in a glass case in a nearby studio. Soon afterwards the studio was almost completely burnt out in a fire, except for the cat

The studio was almost completely burnt out in a fire, except for the cat and its container which weren't even singed.

and its container which weren't even singed. When the cat was taken to a farm, the building was gutted - but again the cat escaped unscathed. A few weeks later a new roof at the hotel caved in, and cost ten thousand pounds to mend. "Then," according to Mr Kemp, "we were just seven days from completion when one of the original beams shifted for no apparent reason. It cost £60,000 to make it safe - but the most spine-chilling part was that the beam was at the spot where we found the cat." The new owners, Rowton House Hotels, decided enough was enough, and a special board meeting gave the go-ahead for the cat to be reburied in the hotel. A vicar was asked to attend the funeral at the animal's old resting place - and the hotel company placed a note on the coffin apologising to the cat for disturbing it, and hoping that it would now rest in peace. Their hopes were realised - everything started to go smoothly again, and the builders caught up so much lost time they found themselves ahead of schedule!

Cat and eagle do battle in Japan

Whether in worlds beyond or times present, cats seem determined to extend their influence over the lives of those around them. Their tactics are usually fairly passive and subtle, but occasionally they leap out of character - whether through bravery, stupidity or sheer bloodymindedness we shall never know. In 1987, a Japanese photographer snapped a cat springing on a sea eagle at the Okayama Bird Reserve. Such feline ambition was not to be rewarded. The Gamma news agency spared catlovers too many details, reporting simply that "this extraordinary event of nature at work ended in favour of the eagle".

David Golsworthy's cat Smokey was rather more successful. So successful, in fact, that he was taken to court, accused, as the *Daily Mirror* put it, of "causing GDH - grievous doggily harm". At the receiving end of the alleged violence was Sheba, a cross between a labrador and a collie. Her owner Mark Castley said that Smokey "just shot out of the bushes and ripped into Sheba. She was screaming and terrified. Her foot pads were ripped off, and there was blood everywhere." The vet's bill came to five hundred pounds, and Mark sued in Aldershot County Court to try to get his money back. David thought a more likely explanation was that Mark's two dogs went for his cat, and one accidentally bit the other. "Smokey," he insisted, is "stupid, very passive, and likes being fussed over." The case - still to be resolved as this book went to press - prompted the *Mirror* to start an investigation to see just how tough cats could be. It asked its readers, "Do you own a monster moggy? Can your fiery feline match - or better - Smokey's story? If your pushy pussy has the neighbourhood dogs on the run, we want to hear about it." And hear about it they did, coming up with a creature they headlined as "Britain's most menacing moggy" - Bruno, named after the heavyweight boxer, Frank.

He was taken to court accused of "causing GDH – grievous doggily harm".

Bruno doing his best to look really mean.

He apparently ambushed a pensioner's two dogs every time she tried to take them out; frightened the labrador belonging to his owner, Janet Harris, and saw off her mother's big crossbreed that normally eats alsatians for breakfast; and terrorised the hounds of a lady from the Cat Protection League, who eventually gave up trying to tame him. As if that wasn't enough to win Bruno the title, Janet added graphically, "There's a piece missing out of one ear, half his teeth are broken, and he's blind in one eye after a fight. He's quite a bruiser."

Occasionally, kindly owners whose cats display killer instincts

Baby Jonathan on the lookout for intruders.

will take the trouble to warn neighbours and other callers. The Absalom family in Cheshire had a blue, longhaired tabby called "Baby Jonathan" who was an expert at seeing off intruding dogs. So up on the front gate went a large warning notice - "These premises are patrolled by an attack cat".

The residents of a quiet crescent at Farnham in Surrey went on red alert whenever Joan Howkins's cat, Maxie, a twenty-five pound tomcat, was out on the prowl. A hardened veteran of street fighting in Aden, weaned on scrapping with alley cats for his food, he'd been brought back by a British soldier at the end of a tour of duty. Neighbour Evelyn Pearce complained, "It's been a reign of terror since Maxie came here. One day our Siamese cat Roger came home with his stomach ripped, and Maxie even knocked a panel out of our door trying to get at the other cats. He is enormous. Our cats weigh fifteen pounds, but they haven't a hope against Maxie." So the two neighbours negotiated a handy way out of trouble. Mrs Howkins puts a red cloth on her washing line when Maxie goes out - and Mrs Pearce hangs up a watering can in her greenhouse when Roger and her other cat, Scissors, go out.

If they had but known it, some gentle music might have saved them all a lot of trouble! The *Daily Telegraph* reported the taming of "Fat Boy", a feline thug who had worked his way through six different homes in the Welsh town of Caerphilly. He was thrown out of each one in turn because of his ferocity, and ended up spending a year in solitary confinement at a cattery - until the Welsh National Opera came looking for a chief rat-catcher for the props department in their Cardiff headquarters. "It was there," they said, "that music finally soothed the savage beast." Fat Boy, it seemed, was a reformed character - "still a fearsome-looking bruiser, but beautifully behaved".

Maxie behind bars.

"Maxie even knocked a panel out of our door trying to get at the other cats."

151

Not so Thomas, whose unsporting behaviour convinced golfing enthusiasts at Weston-super-Mare that a black cat crossing their path was anything but lucky. Thomas appeared regularly at the club's difficult par-four fifteenth hole with the ultimate in course hazards. He jumped out of bushes to grab a golf ball and carry it off in his mouth. After scores of golfers saw the proof of their particularly fine tee-shots disappearing with the black beast, one of them gave chase and discovered where Thomas lived. His embarrassed owner, John Vezey, confessed that the cat had snatched five hundred balls in the previous year. "We've got golf balls in pots, in the wardrobe, in chests and under the bed. I'm sick of it, but I don't know how to stop it." He generously told club members

Chick checks the the hole on the 17th green.

to call at his home if it happened again, and he would hand back two for every one lost.

Players at Redditch town course in Worcestershire had seen it all before. Chick the cat was so adept at snaffling golf balls on the seventeenth green that he even picked them up while they were still moving. And if anyone actually broke through his defences to get the ball in the hole, he had a jolly good go at grabbing that too.

WHAT'S NEW PUSSYCAT?

C ats do not, on the whole, go out to seek publicity for their exploits and mistakes. Indeed, many who delight in being fussed over by their owners are quite embarrassed if a fuss is made of them in newspapers. If you have ever shown a cat a picture of itself, you will know how it pretends not to see the photograph, or simply sniffs at it delicately and walks away with some disdain. But, as with some humans, it is just possible that this is all a front, and that beneath their usually urbane and tolerant exterior there lurks a burning desire for the limelight. In which case, it is advisable that you keep your cat well-informed about the targets it has to top – and some of the bizarre competition it faces – in order to carve its niche in history.

What is left for the mighty cats? What surprises, what pleasures, what new heights of discovery and achievement will they have to stretch to in order to continue hitting the headlines as prolifically as they have in the past. New records will, of course, be set. But, record-busting apart, is it possible that there is little more to be revealed in the world of cats – plenty of variations on well-tried themes, but not much that is truly revelatory? I suspect not. Cats are experts in the art of the unexpected. Investigated by humans, egged on by proud owners, prone to accidents, and encouraged by tales of great, disaster-prone and mischievous moggies that have gone before, they will continue to amuse, amaze and delight.

They will continue to make news.